The Art of Proclamation

The Art of Proclamation

The Sermons of Rev. Dr. Donald E. Williams

DONALD E. WILLIAMS

RESOURCE *Publications* • Eugene, Oregon

THE ART OF PROCLAMATION
The Sermons of Rev. Dr. Donald E. Williams

Copyright © 2025 Donald E. Williams. All rights reserved. Except for brief quotations in critical publications or reviews, no part of this book may be reproduced in any manner without prior written permission from the publisher. Write: Permissions, Wipf and Stock Publishers, 199 W. 8th Ave., Suite 3, Eugene, OR 97401.

Resource Publications
An Imprint of Wipf and Stock Publishers
199 W. 8th Ave., Suite 3
Eugene, OR 97401

www.wipfandstock.com

PAPERBACK ISBN: 979-8-3852-6458-2
HARDCOVER ISBN: 979-8-3852-6459-9
EBOOK ISBN: 979-8-3852-6460-5

12/12/25

Unless otherwise marked, Scripture quotations taken from the (NASB®) New American Standard Bible®, Copyright © 1995 by The Lockman Foundation. Used by permission. All rights reserved. lockman.org. Lockman Foundation.

Scripture quotations marked (NIV) taken from The Holy Bible, New International Version®, NIV®. Copyright © 1973, 1978, 1984, 2011 by Biblica, Inc. Used with permission of Zondervan. All rights reserved worldwide. www.zondervan.com

*I lovingly dedicate this book to Izzie Puryear,
who inspired me to be a better preacher.*

Contents

Introduction	ix
Prologue	1
On Wings As Eagles: Isaiah 40:25–31	3
Every Spiritual Blessing: Ephesians 1:3–14	9
Remember Your Baptism: Luke 3:15–22	15
Abiding In the Vine: John 15:1–8	20
The Agape Love Cycle: John 15:9–17	25
The Assurance of God's Plans and Eternal Love: Luke 2:22–40	30
Faith Is	36
The Transformation: Mark 9:2–9	42
Overcoming Temptation: Matthew 4:1–11	47
The Beauty of Humility: Philippians 2:1–13	53
The God Who Abides With Us In Our Transitions and Trials	58
The Wasteful, Extravagant Son: Luke 15:1–3, 11b–32	64
He Has Risen: Mark 16:1–8	70
The Essence of Prayer: Matthew 6:9–13, 25, 33	76
Parable of the Ten Virgins: Matthew 25:1–13	82
The Parable of the Rich Man and Lazarus: Luke 16:19–31	87
The Parable of the Sower and the Seed: Matthew 13: 1–9, 18–23	93
The Wedding Feast: Matthew 22:1–14	98
Bibliography	103

Introduction

THIS LIMITED COLLECTION OF sermons are intentionally simplistic in language, free of confusing theological terms and erudite vocabulary. They are crafted to be understood by an eighth grader to individuals in the winter of their years, but rich in theological depth and meaning. I have learned in my nearly a decade of preaching the Word that proclamation must principally be understood by the hearer to be effective, otherwise it is like a seed that is sown on a path, seeds that are snatched away by the evil one (Matthew 13:18–19). I pray that you find these sermons to be discernable, inspiring and helpful to your spiritual growth and maturity in Christ. May they take root in your soul and bear fruit, thirty-, seventy- to a hundredfold.

Prologue

JESUS IS THE LIVING Word, the *logos*. Christ is the divine wisdom (logos) of John 1, implicit in the universe providing order and meaning to all things. God uses words, the power of language in divine outreach to the world. Dr. William Willimon asserts in his seminal book *Leading With the Sermon*, in this dynamic of the Economic Trinity, God reaches out to creation in revelation through the Word[1]. Because the Lord speaks, preachers speak through the divinely selected art of kerygma.

Words are at the center of the Triune God's creative activity in the world, indeed the cosmos. God uses divine words in Genesis 1 to speak the world into existence. The Trinity establishes the earth upon its foundations, measures the waters of the sea in the hollow if its hand in creative acts through words[2]. Through words, creation takes its form, ex-nihilo.

Although preaching shares powerful words of divine truth and revelation, it is not always gentle in its effects. Preaching must be confrontational as well. It must be willing to challenge conventional epistemologies in modern culture. This often will stir trouble for preachers, even prompting violent reactions from some who take offense to the Word[3].

---

1. Willimon, *Leading With the Sermon*, 2
2. Willimon, *Leading With the Sermon*, 2
3. Willimon, *Leading With the Sermon*, 12

The Art of Proclamation

Preaching is a shared, mutual endeavor in the church. As the minister preaches, congregants provide feedback in many ways, both verbal and non-verbal. In this two way exchange, preachers often get a sense of the pulse and mood of their audiences[4]. However, preachers must have the courage to speak the truth of the gospel, despite desires of censorship within their congregations.

Through preaching pastors have an opportunity to influence, motivate, orchestrate others. However, such influence must be rooted in the Word, which is active and alive, sharper than a two edged sword, cutting through to the division of bone and marrow. Truth telling must translate into action on the part of the hearers. Congregations must not only be hearers of the Word, but doers also.

The primary way that pastors lead is through the art of preaching. In this "auditory, acoustical phenomenon," the church learns through the hearing, the preaching of the Word.[5] This is why the scriptures assert "faith comes by hearing, and hearing by the word of God" (Romans 10:17). This idea comports well with theologian Walter Brueggemann's thoughts on the inspired canon of scripture:

> "The church is not self-generated, but understands itself in terms of special authorization in a script available for steady and attentive reiteration."[6]

The scriptures establish the identities of Christians, helping to conform them into the Imago Dei, Image of God.

We must lead through the art of preaching, deeply rooted in biblical tradition. I am encouraged in my calling as a pastor that indeed my greatest gift in leadership is preaching. I plan on keeping this as one of my highest weekly priorities in completing exegesis of the Word and crafting meaningful sermons that intersect with the lives of my congregants. As Willimon asserts in the forward of his book *Leading With the Sermon* "preaching is a role to which none can aspire, no one can choose." But having been chosen, I must lead with the sermon.

---

4. Willimon, *Leading With the Sermon*, 14
5. Everhard, "Preaching Lab."
6. Willimon, *Leading with the Sermon*, 48.

On Wings As Eagles

Isaiah 40:25–31

[25] To whom then will you compare me,
　　or who is my equal? says the Holy One.
[26] Lift up your eyes on high and see:
　　Who created these?
He who brings out their host and numbers them,
　　calling them all by name;
because he is great in strength,
　　mighty in power,
　　not one is missing.
[27] Why do you say, O Jacob,
　　and speak, O Israel,
'My way is hidden from the Lord,

and my right is disregarded by my God'?
²⁸ Have you not known? Have you not heard?
The Lord is the everlasting God,
> the Creator of the ends of the earth.
He does not faint or grow weary;
> his understanding is unsearchable.
²⁹ He gives power to the faint,
> and strengthens the powerless.
³⁰ Even youths will faint and be weary,
> and the young will fall exhausted;
³¹ but those who wait for the Lord shall renew their strength,
> they shall mount up with wings like eagles,
they shall run and not be weary,
> they shall walk and not faint.
(Isaiah 40:25–31, NASB)

ISAIAH 40:25–31 IS ONE of the most famous passages of the Old Testament prophets, filled with vivid imagery about the majesty and glory of God, the Great I Am. It is often quoted on Christian mugs, posters, and inspirational cards with inspiring images of eagles soaring on the wings of the wind. However, its critical message is what it teaches us about the power of waiting on God, waiting with hopeful anticipation. Those who wait on the Lord are promised spiritual strength beyond human understanding that allows us to spiritually rise up on wings like eagles, in the strength and power of the Holy Spirit.

Before we begin to explore our text this morning, I need to establish it in its proper historical context. Isaiah 40 -56 is a part of what scholars call second Isaiah. Scholars believe it was written by a school of Isaiah's scribes who carried on his prophetic tradition. The second part of the book of Isaiah covers part of the period when Israel was in captivity in Babylon and also the period after Babylon's fall to King Cyrus the Great in 539 B.C, who freed the Hebrews, allowing them to return to their ancestral homes. So these words are written to people in exile, displaced and likely struggling with their faith in the God of Abraham. Therefore chapter 40 is designed to encourage the people of God and remind them of the beauty, love and power of the God of Israel!

As we turn to our text this morning, The Lord reminds the Hebrew people of who He is:

> 25 To whom then will you compare me,
> or who is my equal? says the Holy One.
> 26 Lift up your eyes on high and see:
> Who created these?
> He who brings out their host and numbers them,
> calling them all by name;
> because he is great in strength,
> mighty in power,
> not one is missing.

The Lord reminds the Hebrews of truths they already know from the book of Genesis. The Lord is the One who created all things by the sheer sound of His commands. He points to the stars and reminds them that not only did he create the wonderous stars in the galaxy, but that he also calls them by name. This is extraordinary when you think there are an estimated 200–400 billion stars in the Milky Way alone. This harmonizes well with view of cosmologist Brian Cox who argues that in a universe of 200–400 billion suns, earth is the only place, so far as know, where there is intelligent life and meaning. This I would humbly add, is by intelligent design and will. The Lord of all creation decided earth would be the place where life would come bursting from the mind of God, creating humankind in beauty beyond compare. Earth is the place where God would step into time to bring salvation and eternal life to the humankind, the only creatures made in the moral and rational image of God. This means we are carved out of God's essence, His moral and rational essence. We have an extraordinary potential to make moral and good choices as we live out this life.

As our passage continues the Lord further describes his faithfulness and the beauty of His nature. The limitations of the physical world do not apply to Him:

> 27 Why do you say, O Jacob,
> and speak, O Israel,

'My way is hidden from the Lord,
>   and my right is disregarded by my God'?
> ²⁸ Have you not known? Have you not heard?
> The Lord is the everlasting God,
>   the Creator of the ends of the earth.
> He does not faint or grow weary;
>   his understanding is unsearchable.

The Lord is not a Clock maker God as some have believed throughout human history. He doesn't just wind the world up like a clock, set it into motion, and walk away from what He has created. This was the belief of some who believed in an impersonal Creator who was not intimately involved in the affairs of the world. However, careful study of the scriptures reveals this belief to be severely flawed. Israel's way is not hidden from God. He doesn't callously disregard the desire and hope of his people! God is everlasting, He is the God who is, who was and is to come. God is everlasting, lasting throughout the vast span of human history. He is not subject to growing weary and tired. Who can fathom his ways? Brothers and sister, these are vital truths to remember! The same god who hung the stars in the Milky Way loves and cares about you. He cares so much that he has numbered every hair on your head. There isn't anything about you with which He is not intimately acquainted. This is why the psalmist says:

> You have searched me, Lord,
>   and you know me.
> ² You know when I sit and when I rise;
>   you perceive my thoughts from afar.
> ³ You discern my going out and my lying down;
>   you are familiar with all my ways.
> ⁴ Before a word is on my tongue
>   you, Lord, know it completely.
> ⁵ You hem me in behind and before,
>   and you lay your hand upon me.
> ⁶ Such knowledge is too wonderful for me,
>   too lofty for me to attain. (Psalm 139: 1–6 NIV)

Yes, the Lord knows our thoughts, even before we form words, symbols to express them to the world! Be reassured that the One who cares, will move on your behalf and aid you in your time of trouble.

As our passage concludes, the writer says:

> [29] He gives power to the faint,
>   and strengthens the powerless.
> [30] Even youths will faint and be weary,
>   and the young will fall exhausted;
> [31] but those who wait for the Lord shall renew their strength,
>   they shall mount up with wings like eagles,
> they shall run and not be weary,
>   they shall walk and not faint.

God gives supernatural power to the faint. He strengthens those who lack power. If we wait, if we look to God with great anticipation that He will move on our behalf, He will renew our strength. We shall mount up with wings like eagles, we will run and not be weary, we will run and not faint. Interestingly, the Lord uses the metaphor of an eagle's wings and flight to illustrate this truth. Did you know that average wingspan of an eagle is 6–7.5 ft? The strength of the bird allows it to dive toward the ground at speeds of up to 100 miles per hour. Its powerful wings allow it to quickly regain altitude once it has captured its intended target. What an incredible metaphor of the spiritual strength God promises his children! When we are weary, He will renew our strength, not just in a mild manner. God will give us incredible strength and flight, just like an eagle.

A few of years ago I was talking to one of my fellow doctoral students about our dissertations. She said to me. "My, isn't God blessing you in your health challenges. He's given you access to therapies and treatments to help you. You're far ahead of everyone in your research and writing. Despite your trials, the Lord has been with you, showing His power and might in your life." In many ways she described the empowering of God that we see in this passage. The Lord allowed me to not grow weary but sour with the wings of eagles.

The Art of Proclamation

My brothers and sisters, I know that some of you are weary. Life's trials and tribulations have beat on the door of your soul and left you weary and discouraged. But Isaiah reminds us that there is hope. We need to wait on the Lord, to wait with expectant enthusiasm that he will hear us, an aid us in our time of trouble. This is a waiting that involves a positive tension between the present and the possible. Let us wait on the Lord. When we do, we shall experience the fulfillment of His great promise:

> [31] but those who wait for the Lord shall renew their strength,
>   they shall mount up with wings like eagles,
> they shall run and not be weary,
>   they shall walk and not faint.

Yes, we will move from weakness to strength. These promises are sure and true.

Every Spiritual Blessing

Ephesians 1:3–14

³ Blessed *be* the God and Father of our Lord Jesus Christ, who has blessed us with every spiritual blessing in the heavenly *places* in Christ, ⁴ just as He chose us in Him before the foundation of the world, that we would be holy and blameless before Him. In love ⁵ He predestined us to adoption as sons *and daughters* through Jesus Christ to Himself, according to the good pleasure of His will, ⁶ to the praise of the glory of His grace, with which He favored us in the Beloved. ⁷ In [c]Him we have redemption through His blood, the forgiveness of our wrongdoings, according to the riches of His grace⁸ which He lavished on us. In all wisdom and insight ⁹ He made known to

us the mystery of His will, according to His good pleasure which He set forth in Him, ¹⁰ regarding *His* plan of the fullness of the times, to bring all things together in Christ, things [g]in the heavens and things on the earth.[11] In Him we also have obtained an inheritance, having been predestined according to the purpose of Him who works all things in accordance with the plan of His will, [12] to the end that [i]we who were the first to hope in the Christ would be to the praise of His glory. [13] In [k]Him, [l]you also, after listening to the message of truth, the gospel of your salvation—having also believed, you were sealed in Him with the Holy Spirit of the promise,[14] who is a first installment of our inheritance, in regard to the redemption of *God's own* possession, to the praise of His glory. (Ephesians 1:3–14)

ALTHOUGH THE 1ST CHAPTER of St. Paul's letter to the church in Ephesus seems to be the support the idea that God chooses who will be saved and who won't be saved, its focus on this idea is not its most important theme. Rather, closer examination reveals an illuminating text about the abundant spiritual blessings that the Lord lavishes upon His children, as we are adopted heirs in the family of God.

The principle theme in our passage this morning focuses on the lavish spiritual blessings of God in Christ Jesus. When the Apostle Paul speaks of these spiritual blessing in Christ he speaks of an abundance or surplus. It means to receive more than what was expected. As Paul states later in the letter, God is "able to do immeasurably more than all we ask or imagine, according to his power that is at work within us" (Ephesians 3:20).

As we turn to our text, the Apostle Paul speaks of lavish and wonderful blessings that we receive in Christ:

> [3] Blessed *be* the God and Father of our Lord Jesus Christ, who has blessed us with every spiritual blessing in the heavenly *places* in Christ, [4] just as He chose us in Him before the foundation of the world, that we would be holy and blameless before Him.

Here Paul speaks of the Lord blessing His children. This means to provide what is beneficial to us a children of God. The Apostle speaks of good things, spiritual in nature that extend from the Lord to his children such as mercy, divine favor, peace, love, strength, spiritual food strength, joy and goodness. The blessings are part of the realm of the Spirit, the invisible realm that we presently cannot see with our natural eyes. As embodied souls, our spirits are fed and nourished with the spiritual blessings and spiritual food from God. The Lord's desire is that we live a life controlled and guided by the Spirit[1].

As our text continues, Paul speaks of the Lord's election of the Gentiles to become fellow heirs of the promises and covenant of God:

> In love [5] He predestined us to adoption as sons *and daughters* through Jesus Christ to Himself, according to the good pleasure of His will, [6] to the praise of the glory of His grace, with which He favored us in the Beloved. [7] In [c]Him we have redemption through His blood, the forgiveness of our wrongdoings, according to the riches of His grace[8] which He lavished on us.

Contrary to the teachings of some early scholars, this passage is not a passage about the Lord preselecting those who will be saved and those who will not. The Lord did not decide before the foundations of the world what souls would be drawn to Him, therefore experiencing the promise of eternal life. Paul does not speak of individuals in this passage. Rather, he speaks broadly about Gentiles who were chosen, selected to become part of the family of God. This is reflected in the earliest part of the Lord's salvific plan to save humankind. When God chose Abraham, He promised the man of God whom had tested, from his seed all the nations would be blessed. Thus, Genesis 22 says:

> [15] The angel of the Lord called to Abraham from heaven a second time[16] and said, "I swear by myself, declares the Lord, that because you have done this and have not

---

1. Discovery Bible, Version 3.0.0, Embros Program

withheld your son, your only son, ¹⁷ I will surely bless you and make your descendants as numerous as the stars in the sky and as the sand on the seashore. Your descendants will take possession of the cities of their enemies, ¹⁸ and through your offspring[b] all nations on earth will be blessed,[c] because you have obeyed me."

This was fulfilled when Jesus the Messiah came through the Hebrew people as the light of the world and Savior of humankind. In Christ we are adopted heirs, sons and daughters of the Almighty.

Once upon a time in ancient Laodicea that was a servant named Linus who served a benevolent, kind lord named Theoros. However, Linus was in great financial debt to Theoros and feared he would never be able to pay off his great debt to his lord. One day while Linus lamented over his overwhelming debt to Theoros, another servant knocked on his door and asserted "Theoros has summoned you." Linus, certain that his lord was going to demand payment for all the money due him, embraced himself for the worse. When Linus entered the lord's study, Theoros welcomed him warmly and asked him to have a seat. Then Theoros said:

> Linus, thank you for meeting with me on such short notice. As you know, I am a man of great wealth and influence. I am grateful for all the work you have done and continue to do in helping to manage my estate. Therefore, to show my gratitude, I have decided to completely pay off all your debts, to include the money you owe me. Also, because of my love for you, I am adopting you as an heir to my estate. You will have the same rights and benefits of any blood heir of mine. You will inherit my vast riches and financial holdings upon my death. In the meantime, I am giving you a large deposit of your inheritance to sustain you before you partake of your full inheritance.

Linus was dumbfounded and sat in awe of his lord's kindness and love. "But why me" Linus humbly asked. Because I love you Linus- because I love you.

We are like Linus in the parable. Our sins represent a great debt owed to our heavenly Father and Creator. Sometimes we sense this debt to God in our feelings of guilt and shame over the sins we have committed. However, through Jesus' atoning work on the cross, our debt is completely paid and erased! What lavish blessings of forgiveness and kindness that the Lord has bestowed upon us! We have been adopted as co-heirs into the Kingdom of God—our inheritance is eternal and royal.

As our passage continues, Paul speaks of the overarching plan of the Lord to bring all things together in Christ, sealing our hearts with the Holy Spirit as a down payment to our eternal inheritance in Christ:

> In all wisdom and insight ⁹ He made known to us the mystery of His will, according to His good pleasure which He set forth in Him, ¹⁰ regarding *His* plan of the fullness of the times, to bring all things together in Christ, things [g]in the heavens and things on the earth.¹¹ In Him we also have obtained an inheritance, having been predestined according to the purpose of Him who works all things in accordance with the plan of His will, ¹² to the end that [i] we who were the first to hope in the Christ would be to the praise of His glory. ¹³ In [k]Him, [l]you also, after listening to the message of truth, the gospel of your salvation—having also [m]believed, you were sealed in Him with the Holy Spirit of the promise,¹⁴ who is a first installment of our inheritance, in regard to the redemption of *God's own possession*, to the praise of His glory.

The whole of human history is culminated, reaches a climax in Christ, the fulfillment of the Old Testament roles of prophet, priest and king. As Gentiles, we are adopted heirs in the kingdom of God with a great inheritance in Christ. The Lord wants to bless us with an abundance of spiritual blessings. He wants to give us more than what we expect. God is able to do immeasurably more than all we ask or imagine, according to his power that is at work within us.

Come to Christ this day anticipating his lavish spiritual blessings of forgiveness, salvation, peace, love, safety , wisdom, guidance and so much more. Come to the one in prayer who is able to provide for you, far beyond what you imagine, ask or think. Meet with the Lord in the beauty of quiet times, allowing him to impart

His spiritual blessings into your life, as you seek Him in the quiet places of your heart. Come to the God of Life who gives spiritual blessings lavishly, that you might be prepared for every good work.

Although the 1st chapter of St. Paul's letter to the church in Ephesus seems to be the support the idea that God chooses who will be saved and who won't be saved, it focus on this idea is not its most important theme. Rather, closer examination reveals an inspiring text about the abundant spiritual blessings that the Lord lavishes upon His children, as we are adopted heirs in the family of God.

Remember Your Baptism

Luke 3:15–22

¹⁵ Now while the people were in a state of expectation and they all were thinking carefully in their hearts about John, whether he himself perhaps was the [a]Christ, ¹⁶ John responded to them all, saying, "As for me, I baptize you with water; but He is coming who is mightier than I, and I am not fit to untie the straps of His sandals; He will baptize you [b]with the Holy Spirit and fire. ¹⁷ His winnowing fork is in His hand to thoroughly clear His threshing floor, and to gather the wheat into His barn; but He will burn up the chaff with unquenchable fire."
¹⁸ So with many other exhortations he preached the gospel to the people.¹⁹ But when Herod the tetrarch was reprimanded by him regarding Herodias, his brother's

wife, and regarding all the evil things which Herod had done,[20] *Herod* also added this to them all: he locked John up in prison.
[21] Now when all the people were baptized, Jesus also was baptized, and while He was praying, heaven was opened, [22] and the Holy Spirit descended upon Him in bodily form like a dove, and a voice came from heaven: "You are My beloved Son, in You I am well pleased." (Luke 3:15–22 NIV)

On the surface, the third chapter of the Gospel of Luke, appears to be a straight forward account of the baptism of our Lord, the desire of ages. However, closer examination reveals an enlightening passage about the baptism of the Holy Spirit and fire, symbolic of the transforming work the Lord desires to do in all of our hearts and souls. May we all live in a way that we hear the Spirit proclaim "this is my beloved child in whom I am well pleased."

As we turn to our text the crowd is in great expectation that John the Baptist might be the Messiah. The people are waiting, watching for the anointed One, the desire of ages. Could he finally be here, the One of whom the prophets spoke of clearly? Could the coming King finally be here to establish His kingdom on earth, a kingdom based on the principles of righteousness and truth. John the Baptist reveals that he is not the one. However, one will come, who even the Baptist is not worthy to untie the straps of his sandals. He will come with a greater baptism. Thus, John the Baptist says:

> He will baptize you [b]with the Holy Spirit and fire. [17] His winnowing fork is in His hand to thoroughly clear His threshing floor, and to gather the wheat into His barn; but He will burn up the chaff with unquenchable fire."

John's water baptism, foreshadows the baptism of Christians. The principal purpose of baptism is a sign of regeneration or new birth. It is also a vital means of grace, whereby the Lord imparts grace, unwarranted favor upon us in our spiritual journeys as Christians. Baptism is a mark that distinguishes Christians from those who have not received the sacrament[1]. As a sign act, baptism uses various elements such as water and actions to express the love of the Lord for His people.

John the Baptist baptized many people in a baptism of repentance (Luke 3:3–4). It is also sign that we have been born again and renounce the forces of evil in the world. John the Baptist used baptism as a sign of regeneration, a new life, a new beginning. It symbolized the spiritual burial, death to self.

Baptism is an initiation into the faith of Christianity. It provides us with new identities as Christians, followers of The Way[2].

Although water baptism is beautiful indeed, John the Baptist speaks of another baptism that Jesus provides for his children, the Baptism of the Holy Spirit and Fire. This is necessarily an individual ritual, but work of the Spirit in our lives whereby we are continually transformed into the image of Christ. John the Baptist uses an agricultural metaphor to describe this:

> He will baptize you [b]with the Holy Spirit and fire. [17] His winnowing fork is in His hand to thoroughly clear His threshing floor, and to gather the wheat into His barn; but He will burn up the chaff with unquenchable fire.

In biblical times farmers used a winnowing fork to separate grains from their husk. Thus, one commentator says:

> John is describing the winnowing or threshing process farmers utilized to separate husks from grains of wheat. They used winnowing fans (or forks) to toss the harvested grain into the air. The chaff (the unwanted husks) would separate from the grain and be lifted away by the breeze, while the heavier grain would settle back onto the ground. The farmer could then gather the grain and store it in his barn[3].

Although this passage is often interpreted as the Lord separating sheep from the goats, the good from the bad as it related to the

---

1. The United Methodist Church, "Articles of Religion," article XVI.
2. Felton, *This Holy Mystery*, 16.
3. Discovery Bible, Version 3.0.0, Embros Program.

final judgement, there is a deeper truth. This is an important passage about in inworking of the Holy Spirit in our lives, transforming our souls, purifying our characters, burning away the chaff, the unwanted husks of sin and darkness in our lives. The Lord is intent on purifying our hearts and souls that we might be conformed to the nature and the Image of God.

As our passage continues, we discover that John the Baptist was imprisoned for admonishing Herod concerning his evil practices:

> [18] So with many other exhortations he preached the gospel to the people.[19] But when Herod the tetrarch was reprimanded by him regarding Herodias, his brother's wife, and regarding all the evil things which Herod had done,[20] *Herod* also added this to them all: he locked John up in prison.

Brothers and sisters, sometimes the cost of discipleship is high. Sometimes we will suffer persecution for being lights of Christ in the world. The persecutions may come at work, or with our family and relatives. Sometimes in the darkness, they lash out against the light of Christ with us. But we must continue in Christ, for He has overcome the world.

As our passage concludes, we discover that Jesus submits himself to being baptized, not because of sinfulness, but as an example to us all:

> [21] Now when all the people were baptized, Jesus also was baptized, and while He was praying, heaven was opened, [22] and the Holy Spirit descended upon Him in bodily form like a dove, and a voice came from heaven: "You are My beloved Son, in You I am well pleased."

What a glorious scene, as John the Baptist baptizes Jesus, the heavens open and the Father speaks: You are my beloved Son in whom I am well pleased.

Jesus shares the nature of the Father who takes personal pleasure in him for His obedience and faithfulness to his mission to show humankind the Way to the Father. This is why Jesus asserted

"I am the Way, the truth and life. There is no way to the father but by me."

I remember when I was baptized at Bethel Missionary Baptist church during my early middle school years. My Sunday School teacher, a godly man, invited my group of young men to be baptized as an important declaration of our faith to the Lord and the community. I remember being keenly aware that this was the most important decision I would make in my life. I was aware of the holy gravity of it. I was making a decision to forsake the world, to become a citizen of a heavenly kingdom. I intended to look firmly ahead and to never look back.

Through our baptisms, the Lord invites us to live lives that bring joy and delight to the Father. He calls us to renounce the work of evil in our lives and in the world. Jesus calls us to be transformed by the fire of the Holy Spirit-to daily be transformed by into the Image of Christ. Today, I want you take a moment to remember your baptism, to remember that you are follower of Christ, and that the Father has sealed your hearts with the holy Spirit. Let this identity guide you in all that you do and all that you choose not to do in this life. May your identity in Christ inspire you to live in full devotion to the God who loves you beyond measure.

Each of you should have received a piece of paper for you to add your name. After you receive your communion elements there will be a bowl of water for you to place paper. The water is a reminder of your baptism, your new life in Christ.

Abiding In the Vine

John 15:1–8

15 "I am the true vine, and My Father is the vinedresser. ² Every branch in Me that does not bear fruit, He takes away; and every *branch* that bears fruit, He [a]prunes it so that it may bear more fruit. ³ You are already [b]clean because of the word which I have spoken to you. ⁴ Remain in Me, [c]and I in you. Just as the branch cannot bear fruit [d]of itself [e]but must remain in the vine, so neither *can* you unless you remain in Me. ⁵ I am the vine, you are the branches; the one who remains in Me, and I in him [f] bears much fruit, for apart from Me you can do nothing. ⁶ If anyone does not remain in Me, he is thrown away like a branch and dries up; and they gather them and throw them into the fire, and they are burned. ⁷ If you remain

in Me, and My words remain in you, ask whatever you wish, and it will be done for you. ⁸ My Father is glorified by this, that you bear much fruit, and *so* ⁽ᵍ⁾prove to be My disciples. (John 15:1–8, NASB)

THE FIFTEENTH CHAPTER OF John contains one of Jesus' famous "I Am" statements in the New Testament. Jesus claims to be "the vine" and insist that we, his followers, abide in him if we are to truly live. This powerful claim is not just a poetic statement meant to please the listener's ears. It is a powerful claim about how to truly live, and not just exist, bearing the fruit of the Spirit in our lives.

The last place that I lived in California was Sanoma County the home of the Napa Valley wine country. Napa Valley is a famous wine producing region located among rolling hills with over 400 vineyards and 600 wineries. Among these wineries are the Robert Mondavi Winery and the Louis M. Martini Winery. I used to love visiting the wine country with friends and relatives, surveying the thousands of acres of vineyards and stylish wineries. There was a vineyard owned by the Christian Brothers monastery, that was a favorite among the many visitors to the area. There is as a special beauty to vineyards, with their elegant rows of flourishing grapes that draws me. No wonder Jesus used the grapevine as a special illustration of what it means to live, what it means to prosper in this life.

As our passage opens Jesus claims to be the true vine. Here true refers to that which is essentially true, connecting fact to reality:

> 15 I am the true vine, and My Father is the vinedresser.

Jesus' claim suggest that there are other vines, less authentic vines to which we can be connected. Jesus likely is referring to other religious ideas, Buddhism, Shintoism, Hinduism and others. Though these religions offer some measure of truth, they are not the true vine-Jesus is the true vine and His Father is the Vinedresser.

As our passage continues, Jesus says that the Father wants us to be fruitful branches:

> ² Every branch in Me that does not bear fruit, He takes away; and every *branch* that bears fruit, He [a]prunes it so that it may bear more fruit. ³

Oh the spiritual pruning of the Lord! The Lord is so concerned with our fruitfulness that he prunes us, removes things in our lives that don't belong. Maybe it's that private sin of ours, of which we think we are only aware. Maybe its lust, covetousness or lying. The Holy Spirit will move to transform you, prune away behaviors that prevent your spiritual growth, your producing fruit. Thus, one commentator says:

> This means in the natural vine the cutting off of shoots which run to waste, and the removal of every growth, disease which hinders the growth of the branch. It means in the spiritual training the checking of natural impulses and affections, and the removal of everything, even though it be by a pang sharp as the edge of the pruner's knife, which can misdirect or weaken the energy of the spiritual life, and thus diminish its fruitfulness[1].

Here, through spiritual pruning, the Lord works to make us as fruitful as possible. Do not despise the pruning acts of the Lord.

As our passage continues, the Lord makes it clear that we must abide, remain in Him in our life's journeys:

> ⁴ Remain in Me, [c]and I in you. Just as the branch cannot bear fruit [d]of itself [e]but must remain in the vine, so neither *can* you unless you remain in Me. ⁵ I am the vine, you are the branches; the one who remains in Me, and I in him [f]bears much fruit, for apart from Me you can do nothing.

As Christians, we cannot produce fruit apart from the Lord. We must be connected to vine. To attempt this without abiding in the vine is foolishness. Thus, one commentator says:

> The branch of itself is a lifeless organ, and only fulfils its functions when it is connected with the vine. So in the spiritual life, men apart from Christ have no original

---

1. Discovery Bible, Version 3.0.0, Embros Program

source of life and fruitfulness. The true life flows from Him to every branch that abides in Him, quickening by its power the whole man, and making him fruitful in good. The man who lives without faith in God may be said to exist, rather than to live, and misses the true aim of his being[2].

This is why Jesus says, without me, disconnected from me, you can do nothing. Are you connected to the Vine this morning? Are you working to continue your relationship with Christ?
What fruit are we to produce as we walk with the Lord? The book of Galatians says:

> But the fruit of the Spirit is love, joy, peace, forbearance, kindness, goodness, faithfulness, gentleness and self-control. Against such things there is no law. (Galatians 5:22–23)

These are the fruit of the Spirit which all have to do with development, the transformation of our character. John Wesley would likely refer to these as marks of the Christian. Is your life characterized by love, joy, the pursuit of peace, forbearance or patience in trial, kindness, goodness? Are you seeking to be faithful, gentle and a person of self-control? These are the fruit that we should produce in this life. Don't be discouraged if you haven't mastered all of these virtues. We are all on a journey towards perfection in Christ. We may have not masters these virtues, but we should be working on them.
As our passage concludes, Jesus shares one of his most misunderstood promises:

> [7] If you remain in Me, and My words remain in you, ask whatever you wish, and it will be done for you. [8] My Father is glorified by this, that you bear much fruit, and *so* [g]prove to be My disciples.

Many people read this verse and believe that if they remain faithful to Christ that they can ask the Lord anything in prayer and receive it. However, as with much of scripture, the matter is more

---

2. Discovery Bible, Version 3.0.0, Embros Program

complicated than this. I John 5:14–1, tells us that God's answer to prayer is dependent on his perfect will. Ultimately, the Lord answers prayers in accordance with His perfect will. Sometimes our desires align perfectly with the will of God, sometimes they don't. We must be willing to still follow our savior, even when He doesn't give us all the things that we ask for.

Some scholars believe that Jesus probably thought of the symbol of the vine and the branches as he and his disciples crossed a valley on the way to Gethsemane. There likely were vineyards in the valley at the time. If Jesus lived and preached during our time, he no doubt would have been inspired by the hundreds of vineyards in the Napa Valley Wine County. Jesus loved to use images from the natural world to illustrate deep spiritual truths. Are you abiding in the vine, Jesus today? Jesus is the source of all life, strength, fruitfulness and flourishing. Abide, remain with Him this day and He will help you to produce fruit, the fruit of the Spirit in your life. He will transform you, guide you and make you holy. Let us remember the prayer of St. Augustine:

> I beg of You, my God, let me know You and love You so that I may be happy in You. And though I cannot do this fully in this life, yet let me improve from day to day till I may do so to the full. Let me know You more and more in this life, that I may know You perfectly in heaven.
> O Truthful God, let me receive the happiness of heaven which You promise so that my joy may be full. In the meantime, let my mind think of it, let my tongue talk of it, let my heart long for it, let my mouth speak of it, let my soul hunger after it, let my flesh thirst after it, let my whole being desire it, until such time as I may enter through death into the joy of my Lord, there to continue forever, world without end. Amen[3].

---

3. Catholic Doors Ministries, Prayer of St. Augustine."

The Agape Love Cycle

John 15:9–17

⁹ Just as the Father has loved Me, I also have loved you; remain in My love. ¹⁰ If you keep My commandments, you will remain in My love; just as I have kept My Father's commandments and remain in His love. ¹¹ These things I have spoken to you so that My joy may be in you, and *that* your joy may be made full.
¹² "This is My commandment, that you love one another, just as I have loved you. ¹³ Greater love has no one than this, that a person will lay down his life for his friends. ¹⁴ You are My friends if you do what I command you. ¹⁵ No longer do I call you slaves, for the slave does not know what his master is doing; but I have called you friends,

because all things that I have heard from My Father I have made known to you. ¹⁶ You did not choose Me but I chose you, and appointed you that you would go and bear fruit, and *that* your fruit would remain, so that whatever you ask of the Father in My name He may give to you. ¹⁷ This I command you, that you love one another. (John 15:9–17)

John 15: 9–17 is a continuation of Jesus' teaching on what it means to truly live. As you may recall from last week, Jesus claimed that in order to truly live we must abide in the Vine, the life source of all human beings. Disconnected from the Vine, we just exist, we are not truly alive. As Jesus continues his teaching on being truly alive, he argues that we are a part of divine cycle of love. The Father loves the Son, the Son pours out His love to us and we are called to love one another.

Before we begin to explore our text I need to define what Jesus means by love in the passage. Jesus is talking about something that Christians for centuries have referred to as agape love. It's not the kind of love we normal think of as human beings, like romantic love, or brotherly love. Agape love refers to our relationship with God and each other, the way that we live out our lives as Christians. It means to "prefer what God prefers, embracing what God embraces by knowing Him—which (ironically) also includes *hating what God hates*"[1]. Agape love is often defined as unconditional, sacrificial love. *Agape* is the kind of love that is felt by a person willing to do anything for another, including sacrificing themselves, without expecting anything in return[2].

Have you ever heard of the Water Cycle? It's a fascinating cycle that describes the flow and change of water in the ecosystem. Thus, the National Oceanic and Atmospheric Administration says:

> The water cycle shows the continuous movement of water within the earth and atmosphere. It is a complex system that includes many different processes. Liquid water evaporates into water vapor, condenses to form

---

1. Discovery Bible, Version 3.0.0, Embros Program
2. Cerebral, "Agape Love."

THE AGAPE LOVE CYCLE

clouds, and precipitates back to earth in the form of rain and snow. Water in different phases moves through the atmosphere (transportation). Liquid water flows across land (runoff), into the ground (infiltration and percolation), and through the ground (groundwater)[3].

As we turn to our text, Jesus begins to describe an equally important cycle, a cycle of agape love that is meant to lead to our flourishing in this life:

> [9] Just as the Father has loved Me, I also have loved you; remain in My love. [10] If you keep My commandments, you will remain in My love; just as I have kept My Father's commandments and remain in His love.

Here Jesus identifies the vital cycle of love in the world. It starts with the Father who loves the Son and the Son loves us. These are the first two parts of the cycle. It's interesting to note that Father in the verse refers to one who passes on His likeness to His children. Indeed, the Lord passes on His likeness to us. This likeness refers to the spiritual attributes of the Lord. As Christians, we should reflect the love, peace, kindness, patience of the Father. Moreover, Jesus commands us to remain, abide in His love through obeying His commandments. Are you working hard to do the things that Christ says to do? Are you endeavoring to walk in the way of the Lord?

As our passage continues Jesus, says that it's possible to have fullness of joy in this life. It comes from Him:

> These things I have spoken to you so that My joy may be in you, and *that* your joy may be made full.

I don't know about you, but I can use the fullness of joy of which Jesus speaks! It's a joy that comes from the Spirit. It is not dependent on the perfection of our circumstances. This joy refers to God's favor, as He leans into us with blessings.

As our passage continues, Jesus speaks of the final part of the Agape Love Cycle that I mentioned earlier:

---

3. NOAA, "Water Cycle."

> ¹² "This is My commandment, that you love one another, just as I have loved you. ¹³ Greater love has no one than this, that a person will lay down his life for his friends. (John 15: 12–13 NASB)

The final part of the love cycle is that we love each other, following the example of Jesus. As we live in community with one another, we should treat one another the way that we want to be treated. We should prefer what God prefers, loving our neighbor as ourselves.

As our passage continues, Jesus says that he has changed the status of his disciples-they no longer or slaves but friends to him. He has brought them near, brought them into a special relationship of friendship. Our Lord Jesus desires a close relationship with us, akin to the close friendships we have with those we love. It's a friendship cultivated by spending time with one another, enjoying the warm company of the other person.

Next, Jesus says that He has as chosen us to be his children. This must not be confused with the incorrect doctrine of election, associated with Calvinism. No, the Lord choses all of us to repent and come into the arms of grace, mercy and salvation. The Lord doesn't desire that anyone should perish, but that all come to know Triune God.

Love, it should be the defining element of us as Christian. The Apostle Paul reminds us of the beauty and splendor of love:

> ⁴ Love is patient, love is kind. It does not envy, it does not boast, it is not proud. ⁵ It does not dishonor others, it is not self-seeking, it is not easily angered, it keeps no record of wrongs. ⁶ Love does not delight in evil but rejoices with the truth. ⁷ It always protects, always trusts, always hopes, always perseveres. ⁸ Love never fails. But where there are prophecies, they will cease; where there are tongues, they will be stilled; where there is knowledge, it will pass away. (1 Cor 13:4–8 NIV)

The Love Cycle is complete with us, the church loving one another as we are called to love. The Father loves the Son and the Son loves us and we are to love one another.

THE AGAPE LOVE CYCLE

Our ministry initiatives for the year are provide us with excellent opportunities to share God's agape love with others. This year we plan to:

1. Establish a Mother's Day Out program (explore partnership with Shiela Webster's Daycare to accomplish this).
2. Establish Movie Night for the community featuring the seasons 1–3 of the popular *Chosen* series.
3. Establish church sponsored dinners (i.e. spaghetti dinners for the community).
4. Build a Band Initiative—Engage in concerted effort to build a contemporary band for a high energy contemporary service. Relaunch a contemporary service when the band is ready.
5. Target a conservative audience that appreciates a more traditional liturgy. Leverage our strength and experience in this area.
6. Engage Facebook audience more efficiently.

In many ways, these initiatives a bold gestures of love to our community. It's a beautiful way to say "We care about you. We also care about your soul, that you come to know Christ our Savior."

John 15: 9–17 a continuation of Jesus teaching on what it means to truly live. As you may recall from last week, Jesus claimed that in order to truly live we must abide in the Vine, the life source of all human beings. Disconnected from the Vine, we just exist, we are not truly alive. As Jesus continues his teaching on being truly alive, he argues that we are a part of divine cycle of love. The Father loves the Son, the Son pours out His love to us and we are called to love one another. Go love your neighbor and make them smile!

The Assurance of God's Plans and Eternal Love

Luke 2:22–40

²² And when the days for [a]their purification according to the Law of Moses were completed, they brought Him up to Jerusalem to present Him to the Lord ²³ (as it is written in the Law of the Lord: "Every *firstborn* male that opens the womb shall be called holy to the Lord"), ²⁴ and to offer a sacrifice according to what has been stated in the Law of the Lord: "A pair of turtledoves or two young doves."
²⁵ And there was a man in Jerusalem whose name was Simeon; and this man was righteous and devout, looking

THE ASSURANCE OF GOD'S PLANS AND ETERNAL LOVE

forward to the consolation of Israel; and the Holy Spirit was upon him. ²⁶ And it had been revealed to him by the Holy Spirit that he would not see death before he had seen the Lord's [b]Christ. ²⁷ And he came [c]by the Spirit into the temple; and when the parents brought in the child Jesus, [d]to carry out for Him the custom of the Law, ²⁸ then he took Him in his arms, and blessed God, and said,

²⁹ "Now, Lord, You are letting Your bond-servant depart in peace,
According to Your word;
³⁰ For my eyes have seen Your salvation,
³¹ Which You have prepared in the presence of all the peoples:
³² A light for revelation [e]for the Gentiles,
And the glory of Your people Israel."
³³ And His father and mother were amazed at the things which were being said about Him. ³⁴ And Simeon blessed them and said to His mother Mary, "Behold, this *Child* is appointed for the fall and [f]rise of many in Israel, and as a sign to be [g]opposed— ³⁵ and a sword will pierce your own soul—to the end that thoughts from many hearts may be revealed."
³⁶ And there was a prophetess, [h]Anna, the daughter of Phanuel, of the tribe of Asher. She was advanced in [i]years and had lived with *her* husband for seven years after her [j]marriage, ³⁷ and *then* as a widow to the age of eighty-four. She did not leave the temple *grounds*, serving night and day with fasts and prayers. ³⁸ And at that very [k]moment she came up and *began* giving thanks to God, and continued to speak about Him to all those who were looking forward to the redemption of Jerusalem. (Luke 2:22-40 NASB)

THE SECOND CHAPTER OF the Gospel of Luke, the physician is quite revealing regarding Jewish law and its ritual practices of purification and holiness. The passage beautifully illustrates the importance of the Law of Moses in the Jewish culture, a culture caught between the beliefs of Greek and Roman society, and Judaism. However fascinating these cultural elements may be, the most significant element of the text is what it reveals about the assurance of the Lord's plans and eternal love in our lives.

One of my favorite passages in the Old Testament is a promise the Lord made to Israel during the time of the prophet Jeremiah:

> For I know the plans I have for you, declares the Lord, plans to prosper you and not to harm you, plans to give you hope and a future. (Jeremiah 29:11)

This verse assures us that God has good intentions for us even when we are facing challenges. These words were originally spoken to the Israelites who were exiled in Babylon, promising them future restoration to their homeland.

As we turn to our text, we discover that Joseph and Mary are devout Jews, following the requirements of the Law of Moses:

> [22] And when the days for [a]their purification according to the Law of Moses were completed, they brought Him up to Jerusalem to present Him to the Lord [23] (as it is written in the Law of the Lord: "Every *firstborn* male that opens the womb shall be called holy to the Lord"), [24] and to offer a sacrifice according to what has been stated in the Law of the Lord: "A pair of turtledoves or two young doves."

Mary has been careful to follow the requirements of the Book of Leviticus that requires women, after giving birth, to observe a purification period of 40 days, before returning to worship at the temple. The primary goal of purification laws in Hebrew culture was maintaining the health of the people, reducing the risk in the transmission of disease.

Our text also reveals that first born males in Hebrew society received special grace from the Lord. Like the first fruit of the earth, they were dedicated to the Lord as holy. Mary and Joseph provide the required offering of a pigeon and doves to dedicate Jesus to His Father Yahweh. It is a humble offering as opposed to the lamb that would have been required of a wealthier couple.

As our text continues there is a shift in the narrative from the strict observance of the law to God's assurances of His plan and love for humankind. The text says that Simeon, a righteous man, thought to possibly be the father of Gamiel, a famous Jewish scholar, has received word from the Holy Spirit, that he will see the promised Messiah before his death. Upon beholding the Christ child, he proclaims:

> [29] "Now, Lord, You are letting Your bond-servant depart in peace,
> According to Your word;
> [30] For my eyes have seen Your salvation,
> [31] Which You have prepared in the presence of all the peoples:
> [32] A light for revelation [e]for the Gentiles,
> And the glory of Your people Israel."

Joseph and Mary are amazed at all the fuss, the independent confirmation of things they have already been told. When Simeon speaks of the Lord's salvation, he speaks of the transformative effects of walking the Most High, whereby we grow into the likeness, the image of the Most High. Simeon affirms that Jesus will accomplish great things among the gentiles and Israel. He likely only understands in part, but He confirms what he has seen in the Christ child. But Why does the Lord allow these things to happen to Joseph and Mary? It helps them to believe that God is moving in the world! It provides them with hope and faith in God's plans and eternal love for his people.

As the text continues, Simeon blesses the child and speaks words, pointing to the crucifixion of Christ 33 years into the child's future:

> [34] And Simeon blessed them and said to His mother Mary, "Behold, this *Child* is appointed for the fall and [f] rise of many in Israel, and as a sign to be [g]opposed— [35] and a sword will pierce your own soul—to the end that thoughts from many hearts may be revealed.

Jesus' life and ministry will disrupt the status quo of Jewish life in the Roman empire. Many leaders will rise in the new thing that the Spirit is doing in the world through Christ. Many will be made low as the Holy Spirit moves over the earth, lifting up valleys and leveling mountains. Yet, Mary will be crushed when she witnesses the cruel death her son will suffer. A sword of sorrow and pain will pierce her soul.

As the text continues, the Lord provides even more assurances of His plans and eternal love:

> [36] And there was a prophetess, Anna the daughter of Phanuel, of the tribe of Asher. She was advanced in years and had lived with *her* husband seven years after her marriage,[37] and then as a widow to the age of eighty-four. She never left the temple, serving night and day with fastings and prayers. [38] At that very moment she came up and *began* giving thanks to God, and continued to speakd of Him to all those who were looking for the redemption of Jerusalem.

The prophetess Anna's confirmation is further proof of the marvelous things that the Lord is doing in the world! Like Simeon, Anna has been awaiting the salvation of Israel. She speaks of the Christ child as the savior of the world. She recognizes that he will save his people and indeed the world, from our sins.

So what do these assurances, spoken over 2000 years ago mean to us in a country experiencing unpreceded change and disruption? Simeon and Anna's assurances point us to the work of Christ in the world. God is still moving in the world! Jesus is the light who has come into the world, showing us the way to the Father. The Christ child is the Bread of life, upon eating we will never die. The Christ child is the One who stands at the door of our hearts and knocks. If we open the door, He and the Father will come into us an sup with us.

Jesus, is also our helper in times of need. Many Americans, government employees are worried if they will have jobs in 8 months. Many recipients of government aid, who are the most vulnerable in society, are concerned about their financial futures. Remember, the Lord has promised:

> For I know the plans I have for you, declares the Lord, plans to prosper you and not to harm you, plans to give you hope and a future.

THE ASSURANCE OF GOD'S PLANS AND ETERNAL LOVE

People of God, the Lord has good intentions for us, even in the midst of great uncertainty and trial. Hold unto these words every day, recite them daily if you must. Cling to the One who is your hope and peace in the storm, even as the storm clouds gather. Remember, the Lord is with you. He will never abandon or forsake you!

Faith Is

11:1 Now faith is the assurance of things hoped for, the conviction of things not seen.
11:2 Indeed, by faith our ancestors received approval.

11:3 By faith we understand that the worlds were prepared by the word of God, so that what is seen was made from things that are not visible.

11:8 By faith Abraham obeyed when he was called to set out for a place that he was to receive as an inheritance; and he set out, not knowing where he was going.

11:9 By faith he stayed for a time in the land he had been promised, as in a foreign land, living in tents, as did Isaac and Jacob, who were heirs with him of the same promise.

> 11:10 For he looked forward to the city that has foundations, whose architect and builder is God.
>
> 11:11 By faith he received power of procreation, even though he was too old—and Sarah herself was barren—because he considered him faithful who had promised.
>
> 11:12 Therefore from one person, and this one as good as dead, descendants were born, "as many as the stars of heaven and as the innumerable grains of sand by the seashore."
>
> 11:13 All of these died in faith without having received the promises, but from a distance they saw and greeted them. They confessed that they were strangers and foreigners on the earth,
>
> 11:14 for people who speak in this way make it clear that they are seeking a homeland.
>
> (Hebrews 11:1–3, 8–16 NASB)

IN THE MODERN CHRISTIAN world faith is primarily thought of as something that we do, or muster up—trust that we have in the Lord. It's is the result of something we do or initiate. However, an examination of the 11th chapter of Hebrews provides us with a broader perspective. According to the Book of Hebrews, faith is God persuading us of invisible things, the world we cannot see with our natural eyes. God produces faith in us that we may see the world as it really is, a world that has been saved by Jesus, the Son for the glory of the Father. Faith is about seeing with new eyes.

In the Greek language, faith literally means to persuade or to be persuaded. Moreover, it means to come to trust, to have confidence. One commentator says:

> "the Lord continually *grows* faith in the yielded believer, so that they can know what he prefers[1]."

---

1. Bible Hub, accessed 8/5/19

The Art of Proclamation

The central idea here is that is faith is God persuading us of invisible things[2]. God wants us to persuade us of invisible realities. He wants us to see the world with new eyes.

Before we begin our exploration of the text in earnest, I want to provide you with a brief background on what the scriptures teach about the invisible world. The bible teaches that we co-exist with the invisible realm that we cannot see with our natural eyes. It is the realm of angels, demons, powers in high places that are at work in the world. This is why the Apostle Paul says:

> For we wrestle not against flesh and blood, but against *spiritual forces*, against powers, against the rulers of the darkness of this world, against spiritual wickedness in high places.

The scriptures teach that creation is involved in an epic battle between good and evil. It also assures us of the end of the story—Christ one day soon will vanquish Satan and all demonic forces, ushering in the reign of God on earth, the fullness of the Kingdom of God.

If faith is God persuading us of invisible things, just what are these invisible realities? First, the Worlds Were Created By the Word of God. Thus, our text says:

> By faith we understand that the worlds were prepared by the word of God, so that what is seen was made from things that are not visible.

Contrary to some secular theories of evolution, the creation of the universe is not just the result of random or accidental forces of nature. The scriptures teach that the creation of the world, the created order are the result of intelligent design. A close examination of Genesis 1 provides a poetic account of creation with striking parallells to scientific theories. Many scientist believe that the universe began in chaos, in a soup of electrons, protons and gases. They theorize that evolution was set into motion by a "big bang"

---

2. Discovery Bible, Version 3.0.0, Embros Program

and incredible burst of energy. Interestingly, Genesis 1 poetically tells the same story, but in poetic language:

> In the beginning God created the heavens and the earth. [2] And the earth was a [a]formless and desolate emptiness, and darkness was over the [b]surface of the deep, and the Spirit of God was hovering over the [c]surface of the waters. (Genesis 1:1–2, NASB)

Here the writer of Genesis poetically describes the primordial chaos that scientist believe existed before "The Big Bang." The earth is without form, it is void, it is absolute chaos. However, in the Genesis account of creation, it is the Lord who creates, shapes and fashions the earth and the heavens. Like a master artist, he creates land, vegetation, animals, stars, all that exist and proclaims "It is good." Finally, before he rest, he creates humankind, in his own image, that is His moral nature to perfectly reflect His virtue, wisdom and beauty. Yes, God wants to persuade us of the truth of our origins. The universe is not just the result of random evolutionary forces, it is the result of God's intelligent design.

Secondly, the Lord desires to persuade us of the necessity of listening to and obeying him. Thus, our passage this morning says:

> By faith Abraham obeyed when he was called to set out
> for a place that he was to receive as an inheritance; and
> he set out, not knowing where he was going.

This text implies that Abraham had a relationship with God, that he was accustomed to listening to God's voice. It is similar to other famous call stories in the bible, like the call of Moses who heard the voice of the Lord speaking from a burning bush that would not be consumed. This was the famous calling of Moses, a Prince of Egypt, who would go on to become one of the greatest prophets in Jewish history. It also is also similar to the call story of the prophet Samuel, who as little boy heard the voice of the Lord calling him in the night. Little Samuel though that Eli the priest was calling him until Eli explained that the Lord was calling Samuel. Moses and Samuel both listened to the voice of the Lord and obeyed His instructions. Likewise, we should listen for God's voice and humbly follow in His ways.

Thirdly, the Lord wants to persuade us of our future hope, our hope in eternal life and our heavenly home. Thus, our text asserts:

> For he looked forward to the city that has foundations, whose architect and builder is God.

What a glorious reference to the New Jerusalem, promised in the Book of Revelations. The New Jerusalem will be God's design, symbolic of the coming reign of God over the entire universe. Thus, Revelations 21 says:

> Then I saw "a new heaven and a new earth," for the first heaven and the first earth had passed away, and there was no longer any sea. I saw the Holy City, the new Jerusalem, coming down out of heaven from God, prepared as a bride beautifully dressed for her husband. And I heard a loud voice from the throne saying, "Look! God's dwelling place is now among the people, and he will dwell with them. They will be his people, and God himself will be with them and be their God. 'He will wipe every tear from their eyes. There will be no more death' or mourning or crying or pain, for the old order of things has passed away." (Revelation 21:1–4 NIV)

Yes, the Lord wants to persuade us of His plans for creation. Jesus died as a sacrifice for our sins that we might have eternal life in Him. In the New Jerusalem He will be our God and we will be His people. He will wipe every tear from our eyes. There will be no more death, mourning or crying or pain.

Finally, the Lord wishes to persuade us of His strong hand in our lives.

> Therefore from one person, and this one as good as dead, descendants were born, "as many as the stars of heaven and as the innumerable grains of sand by the seashore."

The Lord worked miraculously in Abraham and Sara's life. He allowed them to become pregnant while in their 80's, giving birth to Isaac, from whom came the 12 tribes of Israel. The Lord performed a great miracle in their lives and brought fruitfulness out of that which was considered barren. The scriptures tell us that Abraham's faith was reckoned to him as righteousness.

Whether or not the Lord provides us with the miracles we seek, we know that He is with us in our struggles, in our trials. We are not alone, for he is there to comfort and guide, to give us strength and peace in our time of need. The Lord is near to the brokenhearted.

Perhaps you struggle in areas of your faith. Perhaps you long for faith, to be divinely persuaded of God's truth, the reality of the Lord in the world. The Apostle Paul taught us that our faith comes by hearing and hearing by the word of God. God imparts faith through the hearing and the reading of his living word. Come to church regularly and listen to the teaching and preaching of God's Word, the bible. Stay in the Word of God, think deeply on His living word daily and He will persuade you. Faith is also a gift of the Spirit-pray for this gift.

So as people of faith, what do we do with this wonderful knowledge, understanding of the living Lord and Savior? Jesus answered this well in his parable of the last judgement;

> [34] "Then the King will say to those on his right, 'Come, you who are blessed by my Father; take your inheritance, the kingdom prepared for you since the creation of the world. [35] For I was hungry and you gave me something to eat, I was thirsty and you gave me something to drink, I was a stranger and you invited me in, [36] I needed clothes and you clothed me, I was sick and you looked after me, I was in prison and you came to visit me.'

Church, let's do something radical, let's do something crazy! Let's put our faith into action and feed those who are hungry, give drink to the thirsty, be hospitable to refugees and immigrants, not forget those who are in prison and lonely. Let's use our faith to make the world a better place. Let's build a beloved community where we all can flourish together, regardless of the color of our skin or ethnic origins. Faith is about seeing with new eyes. Let us see with new eyes! Amen.

The Transformation

Mark 9:2–9

² And six days later Jesus *took with Him Peter, [a]James, and John, and *brought them up on a high mountain by themselves. And He was [b]transfigured before them; ³ and His garments became radiant and exceedingly white, as no launderer on earth can whiten them. ⁴ And Elijah appeared to them along with Moses; and they were talking with Jesus. ⁵ Peter responded and *said to Jesus, "Rabbi, it is good that we are here; let's make three [c]tabernacles, one for You, one for Moses, and one for Elijah." ⁶ For he did not know how to reply; for they became terrified. ⁷

THE TRANSFORMATION

> Then a cloud [d]formed, overshadowing them, and a voice [e]came out of the cloud: "This is My beloved Son; [f]listen to Him!" ⁸ And suddenly they looked around and saw no one with them anymore, except Jesus alone.
> ⁹ As they were coming down from the mountain, He gave them orders not to relate to anyone what they had seen, [g]until the Son of Man rose from the dead. (Mark 2:2–9)

THE STORY OF THE transformation of Christ is one of the most intriguing stories in the gospels. It is a story filled with holy mystery and wonder as Jesus' appearance is radically transformed before Peter, James and John. The disciples understandably react with both wonder and fear, as they watch their Rabbi transformed before them. But why does Jesus transform himself before his inner circle of disciples? What was the goal of this extraordinary act?

Transformation-it's the chief theme in our scriptural passage this morning. It refers to the major change of something in keeping with inner reality. The natural world provides us with wonderful examples of such change: Caterpillars experience transformation when they build cocoons, only to emerge as beautiful winged butterflies. Tadpoles experience transformation as they transform into frogs.

As we turn to our text, it has only been a few day since Jesus' feeding of the five thousand. The disciples witnessed an extraordinary miracle of Jesus transforming two fish and five loaves a bread into thousands of fish and loaves to satisfy the hunger of the crowd. It was a great sign of Jesus' prophetic ministry. The hand of the Lord was undoubtedly upon him. How else can a man perform such miracles?

As our text continues, Jesus takes Peter, James and John with up a high mountain for an experience that will forever change their lives:

> ²And He was transfigured before them; ³ and His garments became radiant and exceedingly white, as no launderer on earth can whiten them. ⁴

Many scholars believe that the mountain was the magnificent Mt. Hermon in Palestine. Thus, one commentator says:

> The Sidonians called it Sirion = *"breastplate,"* a name suggested by its rounded glittering top, when the sun's rays are reflected by the snow that covers it. It was also called Sion = *"the elevated,"* and is now known as *"the chief mountain."* "In whatever part of Palestine the Israelite turned his eye northward, Mount Hermon was there terminating the view[1].

It is in this extraordinary place, a place known for worship of the gods that Jesus is transformed before Peter, James and John. Jesus' outer garments become a dazzling white, whiter than any soap can possibly make them. In the bible the color white is symbolic of purity, holiness. This harmonizes well with a description of Jesus in the Book of Revelations:

> [14] His head and his hairs were white like wool, as white as snow; and his eyes were as a flame of fire;
> [15] And his feet like unto fine brass, as if they burned in a furnace; and his voice as the sound of many waters.
> (Revelation 1: 14–15)

Jesus' transformation is a change in keeping with an inner reality. But why does Jesus allow the three to see him this way? What is the purpose?

As our story continues, the drama becomes more intriguing. The prophets Moses and Elijah appear before Jesus and begin talking with him. This must have been astonishing! Moses, the Law Giver was there speaking with Jesus. It was Moses who heard the voice of God in the flames of the burning bush that would not be consumed. It was Moses who lifted his rod and parted the waters of the Red Sea, as the Egyptians closed in on the Hebrews. Elijah, was there as well-Elijah who performed great miracles and was caught up to heaven in a chariot of fire. Peter James and John are frightened by the whole experience. Peter awkwardly offers to build three tents, booths for the men, remembering the dessert

---

1. Discovery Bible, Version 3.0.0, Embros Program

THE TRANSFORMATION

wanderings of the Hebrew people. But why does Jesus allow the three to see him this way? What is the purpose?

As our text concludes, The Lord speaks from the heavens:

> Then a cloud formed, overshadowing them, and a voice came out of the cloud, "This is My beloved Son, listen to Him!" [8] All at once they looked around and saw no one with them anymore, except Jesus alone.
> [9] As they were coming down from the mountain, He gave them orders not to relate to anyone what they had seen, [¹until the Son of Man rose from the dead.]

The Father affirms that Jesus is His son, "This is my beloved Son with whom I am well pleased." The disciples are given a glimpse of a mystery about the nature of God. Jesus is a divine being and we are told to listen to him. It's an attentive listening that allows for the birthing of faith within. Jesus said, "my sheep listen to my voice, and I know them, and they follow me"(John 10:27–28). So why does Jesus allow the three to see him this way? What is the purpose? Jesus allows his disciples to see him in His divine glory, His radiance because it is an important confirmation of His divinity! Jesus is the Son of God, the god of all creation who has come to earth to redeem us from slavery to sin. Jesus is the beginning and the end, all things were created through Him. Jesus said if you have seen me, you have seen the Father (John 14:9). Moreover, Jesus transformation is symbolic of the spiritual transformation to which all Christians are called. The statement by St. Athanasius of Alexandria, "The Son of God became man, that we might become *like* god indicates the concept beautifully. II Peter 1:4 says that we have become " . . . partakers of God's nature." Jesus has come that we might become like God in all of our ways.

And so it is that the transformation of Jesus is symbolic of a powerful transformation of our inner beings. Jesus doesn't save us to leave us as He found us. When we become born again, new creations, we embark on a the greatest adventure of our lives, an adventure in the Spirit of the renewal of our minds in Christ, the conforming of our natures to the nature of God. Jesus became flesh, a little baby to help us realize the full potential of who were meant to be. Left to our own devices in this life, we are creatures hopelessly enslaved to sin. Our sin natures often rule us. Our lives are often characterized by what the bible calls the works of the flesh:

- hatred, strife, and jealousy
- fits of anger and outbursts of revenge
- carousing and revelries
- divisions
- adultery, sleeping with people we're not married to
- lust, pornography
- the worship anything or anyone before God
- witchcraft

This is not what we are called to in this life. The Lord calls us to be holy as he is holy. The Lord will transform us and make us like himself if we walk with him, trust Him. He will daily transform us through the power of the Holy Spirit. So stay close to Christ, study the bible daily, pray daily, learn the practice of fasting and prayer, and he will transform you over time. Let us remember St. Augustine's beautiful prayer for transformation:

> Look upon us, O Lord,
> and let all the darkness of our souls
> vanish before the beams of thy brightness.
> Fill us with holy love,
> and open to us the treasures of thy wisdom.
> All our desire is known unto thee,
> therefore perfect what thou hast begun,
> and what thy Spirit has awakened us to ask in prayer.
> We seek thy face,
> turn thy face unto us and show us thy glory.
> Then shall our longing be satisfied,
> and our peace shall be perfect.
> (Augustine, 354—430)[2]

---

2. Just Prayer, "Look Upon Us."

Overcoming Temptation

Matthew 4:1–11

4 Then Jesus was led up by the Spirit into the wilderness to be tempted by the devil. ² And after He had fasted for forty days and forty nights, He [a]then became hungry. ³ And the tempter came and said to Him, "If You are the Son of God, command that these stones become bread." ⁴ But He answered and said, "It is written: 'Man shall not live on bread alone, but on every word that comes out of the mouth of God.'"
⁵ Then the devil *took Him along into the holy city and had Him stand on the pinnacle of the temple, ⁶ and he *said to Him, "If You are the Son of God, throw Yourself down; for it is written:

> 'He will give His angels orders concerning You';
> and 'On *their* hands they will lift You up,
> So that You do not strike Your foot against a stone.'"
> ⁷ Jesus said to him, "[b]On the other hand, it is written:
> 'You shall not put the Lord your God to the test.'"
> ⁸ Again, the devil *took Him along to a very high mountain and *showed Him all the kingdoms of the world and their glory; ⁹ and he said to Him, "All these things I will give You, if You fall down and [c]worship me." ¹⁰ Then Jesus *said to him, "Go away, Satan! For it is written: 'You shall worship the Lord your God, and [d]serve Him only.'"
> ¹¹ Then the devil *left Him; and behold, angels came and *began to* serve Him. (Matthew 4:1–11, NASB)

MODERN SOCIETY IS FULL of many kinds of temptations. Every day we swim in the oceans of consumerism where we are encouraged to pursue earthly riches and glory, often prioritizing riches over family and friends. Moreover, on the internet, we are exposed to high amounts of sexual images and videos tempting us to disobey the Lord's holy commands. But how can we resist the many temptations that come our way every week? How can we live holy and pure lives in a society obsessed with riches and sex?

As we turn to our text this morning, we discover that Jesus our Lord, is led by the Spirit, to be tempted the Devil. Thus, our text says:

> ¹ Then Jesus was led up by the Spirit into the wilderness
> to be tempted by the devil. ²

But wait, who is this of which the text speaks, the devil? The devil in the scriptures is a real person, a fallen angel. He is a liar, an accuser, one who criticizes and hurts. Satan, an archangel who rebelled against God before the creation of humankind in the Garden of Eden. According to the prophets, Satan led a third of the angels of heaven in their rebellion against God and was banished to the earth, along with fallen angels, demons, that followed him. Thus, the Apostle John says in Revelations 12:

> "Then war broke out in heaven. Michael and his angels
> fought against the dragon, and the dragon and his angels

OVERCOMING TEMPTATION

fought back. But he was not strong enough, and they lost their place in heaven. The great dragon was hurled down—that ancient serpent called the devil, or Satan, who leads the whole world astray. He was hurled to the earth, and his angels with him" (Rev 12:7–9 NIV)

The story of Satan, also named Lucifer, God's most beautiful archangel is well documented. His beauty led to his conceit and his eventual downfall.

Jesus has just completed a fast of 40 days and forty nights, reflective of the Great Flood that devasted the earth during the time of Noah. However, unlike the rains that were a judgment on humankind for their sin, Jesus has not come to condemn but to save, to redeem His creation. Thus, our text says:

> 4 Then Jesus was led up by the Spirit into the wilderness to be tempted by the devil. ² And after He had fasted for forty days and forty nights, He [a]then became hungry. ³ And the tempter came and said to Him, "If You are the Son of God, command that these stones become bread." ⁴ But He answered and said, "It is written: 'Man shall not live on bread alone, but on every word that comes out of the mouth of God.'"

Here Satan comes to Jesus when his body is weak, after his long fast, and tempts him to turn the small stones of the wilderness into bread. Yet, Jesus' answers to the Satan all come from the first two chapters of the book of Deuteronomy, verses which devout Jews carried in small little leather boxes, on their robes. This was to remind them of The Lord's Law, to which many sought to obey. Jesus boldly says that life does not consist only of bread, meat, and other food in this life. We must equally nourish ourselves with the Divine words that proceed out of the Lord's mouth, *his* written Words to humankind, the bible! These words are equally as important as bread. But How can we live holy and pure lives in a society obsessed with riches and sex?

As our text continues , Satan twists the meaning of Psalm 91 a psalm of the Lord's protection, and temps Jesus to do something foolish:

⁵ Then the devil *took Him along into the holy city and had Him stand on the pinnacle of the temple, ⁶ and he *said to Him, "If You are the Son of God, throw Yourself down; for it is written:
'He will give His angels orders concerning You';
and
'On *their* hands they will lift You up,
So that You do not strike Your foot against a stone.'"
⁷ Jesus said to him, "[a]On the other hand, it is written:
'You shall not put the Lord your God to the test.'

Here Satan becomes bolder in His distortion of the true meaning of the psalm. Although the Lord does protect His people from many things, he does call us to exercise common sense in spiritual walks. God can do all things, but we should not purposely put ourselves in danger, expecting the deliverance of the Almighty. But wait Pastor Don, you still haven't answered the question you started with. How can we live holy and pure lives in a society obsessed with riches and sex?

The year 2018 was a great year for Michael, a middle-aged executive with a large bank. Early in the year he was promoted to Vice President in the company and took on greater responsibilities in ensuring the bank's adherence to a wide array of policies and procedures. The recent promotion required him to work yet longer hours and travel at least once a month to business locations in the region.

On a recent business trip, to Seattle, Michael, a married man, traveled with an executive named Teresa who was quickly working her way up the ranks. Teresa was high-spirited, intelligent and a highly valued employee to his division. However, Michael noticed that at times she seemed to be quite flirtatious, especially when they were off the clock in business travel. Teresa was attractive and Michael found himself thinking about her off and on throughout the day. Didn't she know he was married? Didn't she care? Recognizing the potential danger ahead, Michael, a Christian started reminding himself about God's word and the many things it says about faithfulness in marriage. Going forward, Michael was careful to ensure that he only met with her in groups, as much as possible, limiting the opportunity to go astray.

OVERCOMING TEMPTATION

As we return to the text, Satan presents Jesus with his final temptation in the wilderness, the temptation for worldly glory, riches, power:

> ⁸ Again, the devil *took Him along to a very high mountain and *showed Him all the kingdoms of the world and their glory; ⁹ and he said to Him, "All these things I will give You, if You fall down and [c]worship me." ¹⁰ Then Jesus *said to him, "Go away, Satan! For it is written: 'You shall worship the Lord your God, and [d]serve Him only.'" ¹¹ Then the devil *left Him; and behold, angels came and *began to* serve Him.

Here Satan offers Jesus what many men and women long for in this world, fame, power, money. He can have it all, if only he worships the evil one as Lord. As the Prince of the air, Satan has the power to deliver riches and worldly glory. Jesus rebukes him a third time with the living word of God. So how can we live holy and pure lives in a society obsessed with riches and sex?

Brothers and sisters, did you notice that in each of the temptations, Jesus responded by directly quoting the bible, the word of God? Each time Satan tempted our Lord he responded with, "but it is written." Like Jesus, our greatest defense against temptation is knowing the Word of God and proclaiming it in all situations in our life, especially times of temptation. The word of God is a mighty sword of truth against the temptations, attacks of the enemy.

Here are some helpful tips on how to overcome temptation:

- Avoiding tempting situations: Remove triggers that tempt you. For example, if you're trying to eat healthier, keep unhealthy snacks out of sight.
- Distracting yourself: Take your mind off the temptation by doing something else.
- Praying: Ask God for strength and grace to resist temptation.
- Enduring the temptation: Resist the temptation and endure it for the joy set before you.

The bible promises that in our temptations, God is with us to help us. Thus, Paul says in 1 Corinthians:

> No temptation has overtaken you except what is common to mankind. And God is faithful; he will not let you be tempted beyond what you can bear. But when you are tempted, he will also provide a way out so that you can endure it. (1 Corinthians 10:13)

The Lord is with you, even in your struggles, temptations. Like Jesus in the desert, remember the Lord will provide a way of escape for you in your temptations. Remember you are a child of the King, that's He's called you to a royal and holy priesthood. You've got this child of God. You've got this!

The Beauty of Humility

Philippians 2:1–13

2 Therefore if there is any encouragement in Christ, if any consolation of love, if any fellowship of the Spirit, if any [a]affection and compassion, 2 make my joy complete [b]by being of the same mind, maintaining the same love, united in spirit, intent on one purpose. 3 Do nothing [c] from [d]selfishness or empty conceit, but with humility consider one another as more important than yourselves; 4 do not *merely* look out for your own personal *interests*, but also for the *interests* of others. 5 Have this attitude [e] in yourselves which was also in Christ Jesus, 6 who, as He *already* existed in the form of God, did not consider equality with God something to be [f]grasped, 7 but [g] emptied Himself *by* taking the form of a bond-servant

> *and* [ʰ]being born in the likeness of men. 8 And being found in appearance as a man, He humbled Himself by becoming obedient to the point of death: death [ⁱ]on a cross. 9 For this reason also God highly exalted Him, and bestowed on Him the name which is above every name, 10 so that at the name of Jesus every knee will bow, of those who are in heaven and on earth and under the earth, 11 and *that* every tongue will confess that Jesus Christ is Lord, to the glory of God the Father.
> 12 So then, my beloved, just as you have always obeyed, not as in my presence only, but now much more in my absence, work out your own salvation with fear and trembling; 13 for it is God who is at work in you, both to [ʲ]desire and to work for *His* good pleasure.(Philippians 2:1–13 NASB)

THE SECOND CHAPTER OF the Apostle Paul's letter to the church in Phillipi shares one of the most important teachings of Christ in the New Testament—the teaching of the humility of Christ. Jesus' selfless emptying of His glory to take on human form for our salvation, is an example of humility for all Christians. The King of Kings, became a poor man, that we might become spiritually rich. If we are to follow Jesus, we must be like minded, in all humility offering our lives in service of others.

Before we begin to explore the scriptural passage this morning, let's look at the main theme of our passage, humility:

Humility is a character trait characterized by a lack of pride or arrogance, a modest view of oneself, and a willingness to acknowledge limitations and mistakes.

Before the Apostle Paul begins to explore humility in the Christian life, he speaks of Christian unity:

> Therefore if there is any encouragement in Christ, if any consolation of love, if any fellowship of the Spirit, if any [ᵃ] affection and compassion,2 make my joy complete [ᵇ]by being of the same mind, maintaining the same love, united in spirit, intent on one purpose. (1 Corinthians 2:1–2)

The unity of which Paul speaks is based on Christians identifying with Christ. As Christians we are also unified under the Word of

THE BEAUTY OF HUMILITY

God. We share the beliefs and values of our Lord Jesus Christ. He is our Master, who shows us the way of life and truth. Also, as Christians we understand the comfort there is in Jesus, the Messiah. He is the Son who bears our burdens, who brings us peace in life's storms. This is why Jesus says:

> 28 "Come to Me, all [a]who are weary and burdened, and I will give you rest.29 Take My yoke upon you and learn from Me, for I am gentle and humble in heart, and you will find [b]rest for your souls. 30 For My yoke is comfortable, and My burden is light." (Matt 11:28–30 NASB)

Paul also speaks of the beauty of Christian fellowship. Our sharing is in what we hold in common, Jesus Christ, who as one commentator says "connects us together into His very body"[1]. The body of Christ is connected together in love, a powerful love that seeks the things that please God. As Paul continues to develop his argument he focuses on the importance of Christians to regard the affairs of others with the highest regard:

> 3 Do nothing [c]from [d]selfishness or empty conceit, but with humility consider one another as more important than yourselves; 4 do not *merely* look out for your own personal *interests*, but also for the *interests* of others.

Selfishness and pride should not be driving forces in the life of a believer. When we are selfish we act in accordance to our sinful ambitions, our personal gain, no matter the strife it may create with others. When we act selfishly, we put our own self interests ahead of what the Lord has declared as good, right and true[2]. Yes, we must look out for the interest of others in the Church and the world.

As our text continues Paul shares the main idea of the passage, the vital importance of Christian humility. If the body of Christ is to do well, humility must be at the core of our actions:

> 5 Have this attitude [e]in yourselves which was also in Christ Jesus, 6 who, as He *already* existed in the form of God, did not consider equality with God something

---

1. Discovery Bible, Version 3.0.0, Embros Program
2. Discovery Bible, Version 3.0.0, Embros Program

> to be [f]grasped, 7 but [g]emptied Himself *by* taking the form of a bond-servant *and* [h]being born in the likeness of men. 8 And being found in appearance as a man, He humbled Himself by becoming obedient to the point of death: death [i]on a cross.

This is one of the most important passages in New Testament writings about the character of Jesus. It teaches that Jesus existed in the form of God, that He is co-equal with God the Father. Yet, He was willing to humble himself. Yes, Christ emptied himself of His glory to take on human form for the sake of the cross, that we might be brought into relationship with the Father. This is his glorious example of humility for us. He thought of us first and was willing to suffer the humiliation and pain of the cross for our salvation and eternal life.

As Paul sums up his argument, he focuses on the kingship of our Lord Jesus, who is the Prince of Peace, the King of Kings whose kingdom will one day come in its fulness on earth:

> 9 For this reason also God highly exalted Him, and bestowed on Him the name which is above every name,
> 10 so that at the name of Jesus every knee will bow, of those who are in heaven and on earth and under the earth,
> 11 and *that* every tongue will confess that Jesus Christ is Lord, to the glory of God the Father.

Yes, one day all people will acknowledge the Kingship, the authority of our Lord who will rule the earth, indeed the universe in all of His glory. His future 1000 year reign on earth will come on earth as it is in heaven and we the children of God will reign with him. What are some practical ways we can practice humility in our lives as Christians?

- Ask for advice or help. You make people feel valued when you ask
- Celebrate and empower others
- Forgive and seek forgiveness
- Practice the art of listening

- Stay open to feedback
- Accept praise and criticism with grace

The second chapter of the Apostle Paul's letter to the church in Phillipi shares one of the most important teachings of Christ in the New Testament—the inspiring humility of Christ. Jesus' selfless emptying of His glory to take on human form for our salvation, is an example of humility for all Christians. The King of Kings, became a poor man, that we might become spiritually rich. If we are to follow Jesus, we must be like minded, in all humility offering our lives in service of others.
St. Teresa of Avilla said:

> As long as we are in this mortal life, nothing is more necessary for us than humility[3].

Church, lets' truly live as the people Christ calls us to be.

---

3. Integrated Catholic Life, "St. Teresa of Avila."

The God Who Abides With Us In Our Transitions and Trials

7 Now the Lord said to Joshua, "This day I will begin to exalt you in the sight of all Israel, so that they will know that just as I have been with Moses, I will be with you. 8 So you shall command the priests who are carrying the ark of the covenant, saying, 'When you come to the edge of the waters of the Jordan, you shall stand *still* in the Jordan.'" 9 Then Joshua said to the sons of Israel, "Come here, and hear the words of the Lord your God." 10 And Joshua said, "By this you will know that the living God

is among you, and that He will assuredly drive out from you the Canaanite, the Hittite, the Hivite, the Perizzite, the Girgashite, the Amorite, and the Jebusite.11 Behold, the ark of the covenant of the Lord of all the earth is crossing over ahead of you into the Jordan. 12 Now then, take for yourselves twelve men from the tribes of Israel, one man for each tribe. 13 And it will come about when the soles of the feet of the priests who carry the ark of the Lord, the Lord of all the earth, rest in the waters of the Jordan, the waters of the Jordan will be cut off, *that is*, the waters which are [a]flowing down from above; and they will stand in one heap."

14 So when the people set out from their tents to cross the Jordan, with the priests carrying the ark of the covenant before the people, 15 and when those who were carrying the ark came up to the Jordan and the feet of the priests carrying the ark [b]stepped down into the edge of the water (for the Jordan overflows all its banks all the days of harvest), 16 then the waters which were [c]flowing down from above stood *and* rose up in one heap, a great distance away at Adam, the city that is beside Zarethan; and those which were [d]flowing down toward the sea of the Arabah, the Salt Sea, were completely cut off. So the people crossed opposite Jericho. 17 And the priests who carried the ark of the covenant of the Lord stood firm on dry ground in the middle of the Jordan while all Israel crossed on dry ground, until all the nation had finished crossing the Jordan. (Joshua 3:7-17 NASB)

ALTHOUGH ON THE SURFACE Joshua 3 seems to be just another ancient story of promised military victory and conquest, deeper examination reveals otherwise. Rather, it is an inspiring story of leadership in navigating critical seasons of transition and change in our lives. The Lord has promised to abide with us and make a make a way in the trails of our lives. The Lord is with us and will lead us into His spiritual provisions, nurturing our souls with the milk and honey of the Spirit.

One of the chief themes in our passage today is the concept of transition and change. Transitions have to do with thresholds, like when we walk through a gate into a new place. It is the experience of being "between" two different places, a transitional period in an organization, individual life or society.

As we turn to our text, the Lord takes measures to strongly establish Joshua as a strong and inspiring leader in whom the Hebrew people will put their trust. Moses, their great leader has died and now young Joshua, God's chosen successor will lead the Hebrew people in conquering the Promised Land:

> 7 Now the Lord said to Joshua, "This day I will begin to exalt you in the sight of all Israel, so that they will know that just as I have been with Moses, I will be with you. 8 So you shall command the priests who are carrying the ark of the covenant, saying, 'When you come to the edge of the waters of the Jordan, you shall stand *still* in the Jordan."

The Lord promised to exalt Joshua, literally to make him great in the sight of all Israel. This is to establish confidence in Joshua as Israel's new spiritual and military leader. The Lord establishes continuing leadership for the Hebrews as they stand at the gate of new horizons and opportunities. The ark of the covenant, which held the stone tablets of the 10 commandment is symbolic of the Lord's constant presence with Joshua and the Hebrew people. God is with Joshua, ever present, blessing and guiding him. However, the Lord instructs the priests, the bearers of the ark to something counterintuitive to our 21st century thinking. Once in the shallow waters of the river's edge, they are to stop and be still. They must be still and know that the Lord is God. It will be by God's mighty hand that Israel will miraculously cross a mighty river in at flood stage during the harvest.

Joshua obeys the Lord and instructs the priest to prepare to see the wonders of God at work:

> 9 Then Joshua said to the sons of Israel, "Come here, and hear the words of the Lord your God." 10 And Joshua said, "By this you will know that the living God is among you, and that He will assuredly drive out from you the Canaanite, the Hittite, the Hivite, the Perizzite, the Girgashite, the Amorite, and the Jebusite. 11 Behold, the ark

of the covenant of the Lord of all the earth is crossing over ahead of you into the Jordan.

The ark of the covenant is symbolic of the Lord's presence in the lives of the Hebrew nation. Because of His lovingkindness, He will go before the people with the priest. The Lord's presence is a sign that he will not only be with them, but that He will empower them to be victorious in taking possession of the promised land. The Hebrews are not alone. God will fight for them!

As the text continues, Joshua explains to the priest the wonderous miracle that is about to take place:

> 12 Now then, take for yourselves twelve men from the tribes of Israel, one man for each tribe. 13 And it will come about when the soles of the feet of the priests who carry the ark of the Lord, the Lord of all the earth, rest in the waters of the Jordan, the waters of the Jordan will be cut off, *that is*, the waters which are [a]flowing down from above; and they will stand in one heap."

Joshua request representatives of each tribe to witness the miracle the Lord is about to perform. As soon as the feet of the priest touch the water, the flow the water will stop, forming a heap, a wall of water. It will leave a clear path for the Israelites to cross safely. But how will this wonderous work happen? The text says that the Lord, the Creator of the heavens and the earth will "rest in the waters." This is simply another way of saying the Lord will be with them and aid them in their time of need. People of God, sometimes we face great trials but God is saying He will be with us in our trials. We must to be still and know that He is God. He will make a way.

As out text continues, the Lord displays His mighty power and acts, as he abides with His people:

> 14 So when the people set out from their tents to cross the Jordan, with the priests carrying the ark of the covenant before the people, 15 and when those who were carrying the ark came up to the Jordan and the feet of the priests carrying the ark [b]stepped down into the edge of the water (for the Jordan overflows all its banks all the days of harvest), 16 then the waters which were [c]

flowing down from above stood *and* rose up in one heap, a great distance away at Adam, the city that is beside Zarethan; and those which were [d]flowing down toward the sea of the Arabah, the Salt Sea, were completely cut off. So the people crossed opposite Jericho.

What an incredible miracle! The Lord abides with His people and makes a way as many say "out of no way." The Jordan river in our text today is symbolic of a barrier, an obstacle that stood between Israel and their taking possession of the Promised land. It was natural barrier between promise and fulfillment.

What barriers, what Jordans do you face in this transition season in America? Our country is in the middle of a transition from one administration to a new one. Yet we wait in the in the "in between" . What thing or things are standing in the way of you moving into God's promises and opportunities in your life? Perhaps your Jordan, your trial is financial. The financial strains of the present moment have made it impossible for you to envision a future of financial security, let alone prosperity. Perhaps your Jordan is relational, you have tried to make a relationship work but nothing you do seems to help. Perhaps you trial is spiritual, you feel absolutely overwhelmed by the chaos in society. Like the vast Jordan river, hundreds of miles long, vast and deep, trials can seem like insurmountable obstacles in our lives. During our seasons of transition and change we must like Joshua:

1. Remember that the Lord is with you. We are not on our journey alone. The God who created all things indwells us and will guide you.
2. Listen to the voice of the Lord and obey His instructions. Be still and know He is God. He will provide a way forward for *you*.
3. Remember God's promise in the book of Isaiah:

    When you pass through the waters,
    I will be with you;
    and when you pass through the rivers,

> they will not sweep over you.
> When you walk through the fire,
> > you will not be burned;
> > > the flames will not set you ablaze. (Isaiah 43:2)

Above all we must remember that our Lord Jesus died of Calvary's cross to atone for our sins and sins of the world. In Him we have peace with God and eternal life. May the God who saves you from eternal death be with you in your trials part that you might experience His blessings and abundant provisions. Let the Lord abide with you in the trials of your life. He will never leave or forsake you. He loves you more than you can imagine!

The Wasteful, Extravagant Son

Luke 15:1–3, 11b-32

Now all the tax collectors and [a]sinners were coming near Jesus to listen to Him. ² And both the Pharisees and the scribes *began* to complain, saying, "This man receives sinners and eats with them."
³ And *so* He told them this parable, saying, "A man had two sons. ¹² The younger of them said to his father, 'Father, give me the share of the estate that [e]is coming to

THE WASTEFUL, EXTRAVAGANT SON

me.' And *so* he divided his wealth between them. [13] And not many days later, the younger son gathered everything together and went on a journey to a distant country, and there he squandered his estate in wild living. [14] Now when he had spent everything, a severe famine occurred in that country, and he began doing without. [15] So he went and hired himself out to one of the citizens of that country, and he sent him into his fields to feed pigs. [16] And he longed to have his fill of the carob pods that the pigs were eating, and no one was giving him *anything*. [17] But when he came to [j]his senses, he said, 'How many of my father's hired laborers have more than enough bread, but I am dying here [k]from hunger! [18] I will set out and go to my father, and will say to him, "Father, I have sinned against heaven, and [l]in your sight; [19] I am no longer worthy to be called your son; treat me as one of your hired laborers."' [20] So he set out and came to [m]his father. But when he was still a long way off, his father saw him and felt compassion *for him*, and ran and [n]embraced him and kissed him. [21] And the son said to him, 'Father, I have sinned against heaven and [o]in your sight; I am no longer worthy to be called your son.' [22] But the father said to his slaves, 'Quickly bring out the best robe and put it on him, and [p]put a ring on his finger and sandals on his feet; [23] and bring the fattened calf, slaughter it, and let's eat and celebrate; [24] for this son of mine was dead and has come to life again; he was lost and has been found.' And they began to celebrate.

[25] "Now his older son was in the field, and when he came and approached the house, he heard music and dancing. [26] And he summoned one of the servants and *began* inquiring what these things could be. [27] And he said to him, 'Your brother has come, and your father has slaughtered the fattened calf because he has received him back safe and sound.' [28] But he became angry and was not willing to go in; and his father came out and *began* pleading with him. [29] But he answered and said to his father, 'Look! For so many years I have been serving you and I have never [q]neglected a command of yours; and *yet* you never gave me a young goat, so that I might celebrate with my friends; [30] but when this son of yours came, who has

> devoured your [r]wealth with prostitutes, you slaughtered the fattened calf for him.' ³¹ And he said to him, 'Son, you [s]have always been with me, and all that is mine is yours. ³² But we had to celebrate and rejoice, because this brother of yours was dead and *has begun* to live, and *was* lost and has been found.'" (Luke 15:1–3,11b-32 NASB)

THE PARABLE OF THE wasteful, extravagant spending son is one of the most famous stories of repentance and forgiveness. It is a part of a trio of three stories that tell the stories of things that are lost and found. These stories in their totality reveal in exquisite detail that Jesus cares about lost souls, individuals who have lost their spiritual way in this life. Sometimes, we lose our way, we lose sight of Christ our North Star in this life. However, we can take comfort that our Lord will always go the distance to find us, no matter the severity of our sins, to show us the sure way home. Through God's eternal lovingkindness, the Lord makes our Spirits to come "fully alive" in Christ.

As we turn to our text, Jesus establishes the scene for his listeners, a largely Jewish audience. The Pharisees are complaining that Jesus would dare to sit with tax collectors and sinners. Doesn't Jesus recognize that they are lost, unworthy souls with which to mingle? Aware of their criticism, Jesus tells the story of the Prodigal son:

> ³ And *so* He told them this parable, saying, "A man had two sons. ¹² The younger of them said to his father, 'Father, give me the share of the estate that [e]is coming to me.' And *so* he divided his [f]wealth between them. ¹³ And not many days later, the younger son gathered everything together and went on a journey to a distant country, and there he squandered his estate in wild living.

Many scholars believe that the younger son's journey to another land was not uncommon in first-century Palestine. Many were the temptations of youth to venture into other areas of the world to seek their fortunes or pursue worldly pleasures: Thus, one scholar says:

THE WASTEFUL, EXTRAVAGANT SON

The young man left his home, and started, bent on pleasure or on gain, for Alexandria, or Rome, or Corinth, and rumor came home of riotous living, and a fortune wasted upon prostitutes, sabbaths broken, synagogues unvisited, perhaps even of participation in idol feasts. In the interpretation that lies below the surface, the "far country" is the state of the human spirit, of the Gentile world, in their wanderings far off from God. The *"wild living"* is the reckless waste of noble gifts and highest energies on *sexual pleasures* of life, or and the worship of false gods[1].

As our passage continues the young son, now broke and lacking the basic necessities of life, must figure out a way to survive in a foreign land:

> Now when he had [h]spent everything, a severe famine occurred in that country, and he began doing without. 15 So he went and [i]hired himself out to one of the citizens of that country, and he sent him into his fields to feed pigs. 16 And he longed to have his fill of the carob pods that the pigs were eating, and no one was giving him *anything.*

For the Jews listening to the story, the young son's difficult situation must have seemed horrifying. Swine were unclean in the Jewish dietary system, and they were not allowed to consume them. His feeding the pigs must have been a mirror of his unclean soul, which inspired bad decisions that led to his present predicament.

As our passage continues, the son's eyes are finally opened:

> But when he came to [j]his senses, he said, 'How many of my father's hired laborers have more than enough bread, but I am dying here [k]from hunger! 18 I will set out and go to my father, and will say to him, "Father, I have sinned against heaven, and [l]in your sight; 19 I am no longer worthy to be called your son; treat me as one of your hired laborers."

---

1. Discovery Bible, Version 3.0.0, Embros Program

The younger son realizes the error of his ways and becomes truly repentant for his behavior. He is ready to humble himself and work as a servant for his kind father. Thus, one scholar says:

> I will arise and go to my father.—This, then, was the first fruits of repentance. He remembers that he has a father, and trusts in that father's love; but he dares not claim the old position which he had so recklessly cast away. He is content to be as one of the "hired servants. Spiritually, the first impulse of the repentant heart is to take the lowest place, to wish for the drudgery of daily duties, or even menial service, if only it may be near its Father in heaven, and by slow degrees regain His favor and earn the wages of His praises in as virtually including all that grew out of it."

And so it is, that we should remember the necessity of confession and contrite hearts when we sin. The Father is faithful to forgive us and cleanse us from all unrighteousness.

The drama of the parable comes to a glorious climax as the son sets out on his journey home:

> But when he was still a long way off, his father saw him and felt compassion *for him*, and ran and [n]embraced him and kissed him. [21] And the son said to him, 'Father, I have sinned against heaven and [o]in your sight; I am no longer worthy to be called your son.' [22] But the father said to his slaves, 'Quickly bring out the best robe and put it on him, and [p]put a ring on his finger and sandals on his feet;[23] and bring the fattened calf, slaughter it, and let's eat and celebrate; [24] for this son of mine was dead and has come to life again; he was lost and has been found.' And they began to celebrate.

The father in the parable, symbolic of our Heavenly Father, rejoices that his rebellious son has returned. The young son repents for his behavior and is truly sorrowful for the choices he has made. The father celebrates the son's transition from death to new life. His son was spiritually dead, powerless, unresponsive to life-giving influences. However, now he is alive. The son's spiritual awakening is enabling him to become fully alive as he learns to walk in wisdom.

In many ways, this story is a tale about us. Sometimes, we lose our way, we lose sight of Christ our North Star in this life. However, we can take comfort that our Lord will always go the distance to find us, no matter the severity of our sins, to show us the sure way home. Through God's lovingkindness, He makes our Spirits to come "fully alive" in Christ.

Maybe you are a wasteful son, or daughter and you have lost your way spiritually. When you left home, you left the values and the Christian faith that you were baptized into as a child and confirmed through confirmation experience. Perhaps your youthful journey led to wild living and the pursuit of pleasure. But like the young son in the parable, it all left you bankrupt and broken. The Spirit says, come home my daughter, my son-come home. Come home to the One who knew you before you were formed in your mother's womb. Come home to the God who knows your name and has written it on the palm of His hand. Come home to the God who endured Calvary's cruel cross, to pay the debt for your sins and to give you eternal life. Take comfort that Our Lord will always go the distance to find you, no matter your sins, to show you the sure way home. Through love, God will make your spirit to come "fully alive" in Christ. Like the loving father in the story, when you return the father will come running out to greet and embrace you with open arms. He will always welcome you home!

He Has Risen

Mark 16:1–8

16 When the Sabbath was over, Mary Magdalene, Mary the *mother* of [a]James, and Salome bought spices so that they might come and anoint Him. ² And very early on the first day of the week, they *came to the tomb when the sun had risen. ³ They were saying to one another, "Who will roll away the stone from the entrance of the tomb for us?" ⁴ And looking up, they *noticed that the stone had been rolled away; [b]for it was extremely large. ⁵ And entering the tomb, they saw a young man sitting at the right, wearing a white robe; and they were amazed. ⁶ But he *said to them, "Do not be amazed; you are looking for Jesus the Nazarene, who has been crucified. He has risen; He is not here; see, *here is* the place where they laid

Him. ⁷ But go, tell His disciples and Peter, 'He is going ahead of you to Galilee; there you will see Him, just as He told you.'" ⁸ And they went out and fled from the tomb, for trembling and astonishment had gripped them; and they said nothing to anyone, for they were afraid. (Mark 16:1–8 NASB)

NO EVENT HAS HAD such a major influence on the arch of human history than the resurrection of Jesus Christ, the Messiah. The resurrection of the God/Man from Nazareth, who represented the Old Testament offices of Prophet, Priest and King has spread throughout the world establishing a major religion whose influence has reached nearly every corner of the inhabited world. The resurrection will be celebrated in over 95 countries this Easter by an international group of Christians who bear the image and name of Christ. But, I wonder, what is the meaning of the resurrection?

To understand the meaning of the resurrection we must step back in time to the origins of humankind, after God established the earth upon its foundations, measured the waters of the seas in the hollow of His hand and fashioned His greatest creation, humankind. After creating Adam in the image of God, that is the moral and rational image of Himself, God gave Adam special instructions:

> ¹⁵ The Lord God took the man and put him in the Garden of Eden to work it and take care of it. ¹⁶ And the Lord God commanded the man, "You are free to eat from any tree in the garden; ¹⁷ but you must not eat from the tree of the knowledge of good and evil, for when you eat from it you will certainly die." (Genesis 2:15–17 NIV)

As you may remember in the Genesis story, Adam and Eve disobeyed these explicit instructions, resulting in the bodies of humans eventually growing old and dying. Many scholars believe that Adam and Eve were created to be eternal beings, beings that never die. The tree of Life, providing eternal life was in the Garden all along. They were free to eat of it, but did not. However, their expulsion from the garden left them as individuals who would eventually die. But what I wonder, is the meaning of the resurrection?

The Art of Proclamation

As we turn to out text this morning, we discover two Marys, Mary Magdalene and Mary the mother of James, and Salome, who are prepared to anoint Jesus' expired body for burial, in accordance with Jewish custom:

> 16 When the Sabbath was over, Mary Magdalene, Mary the *mother* of [a]James, and Salome bought spices so that they might come and anoint Him. ² And very early on the first day of the week, they *came to the tomb when the sun had risen. ³ They were saying to one another, "Who will roll away the stone from the entrance of the tomb for us?"

Interestingly, John's gospel account reveals something of which they are not aware. Nicodemus has already anointed the body with spices, according to Jewish custom, preparing it for burial. The Father has ensured that His son's body has been honored in the Jewish custom.

As the women look up, they notice something marvelous:

> ⁴ And looking up, they *noticed that the stone had been rolled away; [b]for it was extremely large. ⁵ And entering the tomb, they saw a young man sitting at the right, wearing a white robe; and they were amazed. ⁶ But he *said to them, "Do not be amazed; you are looking for Jesus the Nazarene, who has been crucified. He has risen; He is not here; see, *here is* the place where they laid Him. ⁷ But go, tell His disciples and Peter, 'He is going ahead of you to Galilee; there you will see Him, just as He told you.'"

How can it be that the massive stone has been rolled away? The only person in the tomb is a young man in white, regal robe flowing down to his ankles. Matthew's gospel lets us know this is no ordinary young man. Thus, the Gospel of Matthew says:

> Now after the Sabbath, as it began to dawn toward the first *day* of the week, Mary Magdalene and the other Mary came to look at the tomb. 2 And behold, a severe earthquake had occurred, for an angel of the Lord descended from heaven and came and rolled away the stone, and sat upon it. 3 And his appearance was like lightning, and

> his clothing as white as snow. 4 The guards shook from fear of him and became like dead men. 5 And the angel said to the women, "[a]Do not be afraid; for I know that you are looking for Jesus who has been crucified. 6 He is not here, for He has risen, just as He said. Come, see the place where He was lying. (Matthew 28:1-6)

It is a mighty angel, a bright being whose very presence strikes fear in the hearts of the guards. Heaven has opened and an angel from heaven is working out God's purposes in the world. The angel informs the women that Jesus is not in the tomb, he has arisen, which means *to waken, to raise up*. But, I wonder, what is the meaning of the resurrection?

As our text concludes, the heavenly messenger commands the women to proclaim the good news to Jesus' disciples:

> [7] But go, tell His disciples and Peter, 'He is going ahead of you to Galilee; there you will see Him, just as He told you.'" [8] And they went out and fled from the tomb, for trembling and astonishment had gripped them; and they said nothing to anyone, for they were afraid.

The women are charged with passing on the amazing news of the resurrection to Jesus' disciples. The angel promise that they will see Jesus in his resurrection state. The women are completely astonished, dumfounded by the experience and the news. But, I wonder, what is the meaning of the resurrection? In His resurrection Jesus defeated the curse of death established in Genesis 3. Because of Jesus resurrection, death no longer has power over humanity. This is why Jesus boldly said to Martha before the resurrection of Lazarus:

> I am the resurrection and the life. He who believes in Me, though he may die, he shall live. [26] And whoever lives and believes in Me shall never die. Do you believe this?" (John 11: 25-26)

The resurrection of Christ means that we can share in the eternal nature of God. Jesus' resurrection takes the sting out of death for his children, for we know that the expiration of our mortal bodies are not the end of us. As eternal beings, will live forever, we truly will never die. The scriptures teach that we will receive new bodies that will never waste away. In Jesus resurrection, He invites all to share in His resurrection life where we will dwell and reign with the Living God throughout all time. Most importantly, the resurrection affirms the completion of Jesus' atoning work on the cross to redeem us from our sins. This is why the prophet Isaiah says:

> ³ He was despised and rejected by mankind,
>   a man of suffering, and familiar with pain.
> Like one from whom people hide their faces
>   he was despised, and we held him in low esteem.
> ⁴ Surely he took up our pain
>   and bore our suffering,
> yet we considered him punished by God,
>   stricken by him, and afflicted.
> ⁵ But he was pierced for our transgressions,
>   he was crushed for our iniquities;
> the punishment that brought us peace was on him,
>   and by his wounds we are healed.
> ⁶ We all, like sheep, have gone astray,
>   each of us has turned to our own way;
> and the Lord has laid on him
>   the iniquity of us all. (Isaiah 53:3–6 NIV)

Many of us have become acquainted with death. We have friends and family who have been sickened by disease. We mourn the loss of the ones we love and desperately hope for cures that will prolong life here on earth. Yet, Jesus' resurrection gives us hope in the midst of death and darkness. Death will not have victory over those who believe in Christ and his atoning work on the cross. The end of this life is only the beginning of eternity, dwelling and reigning with the Prince of Peace, the King of the universe. We will live forever with the One who knew us, even before we were formed in our mother's womb. Scripture promises us that you will receive new resurrected bodies that will never die, or succumb to disease. So, I invite you to come, all you who are weary and heavy laden. Follow Christ, learn from Him and you will find rest for your souls. His burden is light. Come this day to the risen Christ who is the bread of life. If you eat this bread, He promises you will never die. Come to Christ who is the Vine, in whom living you will be connected to the one who is life itself, the One from whom all life flows. Come to the risen Christ and live! Christ has risen! Christ has risen indeed.

The Essence of Prayer

Matthew 6:9–13, 25, 33

THE LORD'S PRAYER
9 "Pray, then, in this way:
'Our Father, who is in heaven,
[d]Hallowed be Your name.
10 [e]Your kingdom come.
Your will be done,
[f]On earth as it is in heaven.
11 Give us this day [g]our daily bread.
12 And forgive us our debts, as we also have forgiven our debtors.
13 And do not lead us into temptation, but deliver us from [h]evil.[i]'

THE ESSENCE OF PRAYER

> ¹⁴ For if you forgive *other* people for their ⁽ⁱ⁾offenses, your heavenly Father will also forgive you. ¹⁵ But if you do not forgive *other* people, then your Father will not forgive your ⁽ᵏ⁾offenses.
> ²⁵ "For this reason I say to you, ⁽ᑫ⁾do not be worried about your ⁽ʳ⁾life, *as to* what you will eat or what you will drink; nor for your body, *as to* what you will put on. Is life not more than food, and the body more than clothing?
> ³³ But ⁽ᵘ⁾seek first ⁽ᵛ⁾His kingdom and His righteousness, and all these things will be ⁽ʷ⁾provided to you. (Matthew 6:9-13, 25, 33 NASB)

THERE ARE MANY DIFFERENT concepts of prayer in the modern world. Some regard prayer as simply a way of communing with the divine. Others regard it as way of petitioning the Lord to get our heartfelt desires fulfilled. Although all of these are noble and true realities, Luke's gospel provides a deeper understanding of prayer. According to the Gospel of Luke, the essence of prayer is found in aligning our desires with God's desires and His ultimate purposes in the world. When one of the disciples asks Jesus to teach them to pray, the word for prayer literally means to exchange our wishes for God's wishes. It is the same word that is used when the text says that Jesus was praying to the Father. The Son of God, was ensuring that his desires were in perfect harmony with the Father. Ultimately, prayer is about aligning our desires with God's desires.

Before we begin to explore these beautiful truths in the Lord's prayer, I want to talk to you about tire alignments on vehicles. A tire alignment enables your car to tires to function properly. In fact a tire alignment effects the overall function and efficiency of your car. Dear I say, God wants to give all of our souls spiritual alignments.

The Lord's prayer helps us to recognize several critical truths about God. First, the Lord's prayer helps us to recognize the holiness of God. This is why it begins with these beautiful words:

"Father, hallowed is your name"

Our heavenly Father is holy and he calls us to be holy like himself. His very name is holy. God's holiness means He is separate from all other things. He is utterly pure like fresh mountain waters. The Lord is unique, there is no one like him. The Lord is separate from sin, moral evil. He is the perfect reflection of morality and virtue. God is above and beyond the limitations of the physical world and humanity. God cannot tolerate sin and is repulsed by it. Because God is holy, He calls on us to strive for holiness in their lives, to be set apart for His purposes. Essentially, God's holiness is the core of His divine nature. The Lord's holiness inspires us to worship Him, to be in awe of His beauty[1].

Secondly, prayer helps us to recognize we are citizens of another kingdom, the Kingdom of God. Thus, in Jesus' pattern of prayer he says: "Thy kingdom come."

Jesus taught us that the Kingdom of God is both a present and a future reality. We experience the Kingdom when the Lord of life comes to dwell within us, to sup with us, when he becomes enthroned in our hearts. We acknowledge Him as the Prince of Peace, the King of Kings who has come to take His rightful place in our hearts and the world. Currently His kingdom is not of this world but of the human heart and soul. But as seen in John Wesley's vision of the world, we believe God's mission of salvation will grow like a creshendo, ushering in the 1000 year reign of Christ on earth, the coming of the kingdom in its fullness. Saints, Jesus is coming back one day and He will rule the earth in justice and peace.

Next, prayer helps us to recognize the vital importance of God's will in our lives and in the world. This is why the Lord's Prayer says:

Thy will be done on earth as it is in heaven.

This reflects the meaning of the word prayer in Hebrew-an exchange of our desires for God's desires, an alignment of our wills with God's will. This phrase expresses a desire for God's will to be perfectly and completely fulfilled on Earth, just as it is in heaven. It signifies a prayer of submission and a request for divine guidance in aligning one's life with God's plan.

1. Lindsley, "Holiness of God."

THE ESSENCE OF PRAYER

When we say "thy will be done" we acknowledge God's authority and sovereignty. It's a commitment to align our own desires and plans with God's purposes. This prayer reveals that in heaven God's will is fully carried out. The angels are careful to obey the will of the Lord. The Triune God desires the same on earth, as we are created to love and follow of Creator. When we pray "Thy will be done" we are asking the Lord to guide and direct our lives, to help us fulfill His purpose in our lives.

Forth, prayer helps us to recognize that God is our principle provider in this life. Thus, Jesus' pattern of prayer says:

> "Give us this day our daily bread..."

The scriptures teach that the Lord is the source of all our blessings in this life. He is our heavenly provider, the one who opens the heavens to rain upon our crops. Just as the Lord provided the Israelites with manna daily in their 40 ears of desert wanderings, the Lord provides for us daily. This is why Jesus said:

> Consider the ravens: They do not sow or reap, they have no storeroom or barn; yet God feeds them. And how much more valuable you are than birds! Who of you by worrying can add a single hour to your life? Since you cannot do this very little thing, why do you worry about the rest? (Luke 12: 24–25 NASB)

Furthermore, the Apostle Paul says in his letter to the Church in Phillipi:

> "My God will supply all of your needs according to His riches and glory in Christ Jesus" (Philippians 4:19).

The Lord is mighty to provide for his children and calls us to trust in Him for our daily provisions, for He cares for us.

Next, the Lord's prayer helps us to recognize the vital importance of forgiveness in our lives. Thus, the Lords pattern of prayer says:

> [12] And forgive us our debts, as we also have forgiven our debtors.

¹³ And do not lead us into temptation, but deliver us from [h]evil.[i]'

Our Lord is a God of peace and requires us to seek His forgiveness for our sins and in return extend forgiveness to those who sin against us. Forgiveness in the Greek means to send away, to release any desire to punish, take revenge on others. When we forgive, we release all bitterness and unforgiveness towards others. Church, forgiveness is something we must do as Christians. It is a divine requirement! Forgiving others is so important to God that he tells us if we do not forgive others their sins, He will not forgive our sins. Someone once said "Unforgiveness is like drinking poison hoping you will hurt the other person." It doesn't work and only takes its toll on our bodies and souls.

Jesus' pattern of prayer also reminds us to look to God for deliverance from all sorts of evil in the world. Sadly, the world is full of many evil forces, some spiritual, governmental, racial and economic. Evil abounds-we need God's deliverance from evil.

Finally, we experience this alignment through seeking first the Kingdom of God and His righteousness. Seeking first the Kingdom of God and His righteousness means prioritizing God's will and values above all else in your life. It involves actively pursuing a life aligned with God's character and His purposes for the world. This includes developing a heart for God, seeking His presence, and living a life that reflects His love and grace. We seek first his Kingdom when we are committed to furthering the kingdom of God through dynamics acts of ministry. This involves proclaiming the Good News to the poor, binding up the broken hearted, providing deliverance to those enslaved to their sin, comforting those who mourn.

Luke's gospel provides a deeper understanding of prayer. The essence of prayer is found in aligning our desires with the God's desires and His ultimate purposes in the world. Prayer helps us to recognize several important things:

- The holiness of God and our call to be holy, pure and righteous
- We are citizens of another kingdom-the Kingdom of God

- The importance of the will of God
- The provision of God in our lives
- The importance of forgiveness in our everyday lives
- The importance of looking to God for deliverance from evil in the world
- The importance of making the Lord our highest priority in life

Parable of the Ten Virgins

Matthew 25:1–13

25 "At that time the kingdom of heaven will be like ten virgins who took their lamps and went out to meet the bridegroom. ² Five of them were foolish and five were wise. ³ The foolish ones took their lamps but did not take any oil with them. ⁴ The wise ones, however, took oil in jars along with their lamps. ⁵ The bridegroom was a long time in coming, and they all became drowsy and fell asleep.
⁶ "At midnight the cry rang out: 'Here's the bridegroom! Come out to meet him!'
⁷ "Then all the virgins woke up and trimmed their lamps. ⁸ The foolish ones said to the wise, 'Give us some of your oil; our lamps are going out.'

> ⁹ "'No,' they replied, 'there may not be enough for both us and you. Instead, go to those who sell oil and buy some for yourselves.'
> ¹⁰ "But while they were on their way to buy the oil, the bridegroom arrived. The virgins who were ready went in with him to the wedding banquet. And the door was shut.
> ¹¹ "Later the others also came. 'Lord, Lord,' they said, 'open the door for us!'
> ¹² "But he replied, 'Truly I tell you, I don't know you.'
> ¹³ "Therefore keep watch, because you do not know the day or the hour. (Matt 25:1–13)

THE PARABLE OF THE Ten Virgins tells the story of 10 Virgins, 5 wise and 5 foolish. They are anxiously awaiting the arrival of the Bridegroom who is delayed in his coming. Only 5 of the Virgins are prepared with extra oil for their lamps, in case the delay is longer than they anticipate. But what is the meaning of this mysterious parable? What does it teach us about Christian discipleship?

As Jesus begins his parable, he makes it clear that the parable is really a story about the Kingdom of God. What does Jesus mean when he talks about the Kingdom of God? The Kingdom of God is a both a present and future reality, expanding on the earth through the proclamation of the gospel and the reign of God in the hearts of believers. As the Bread of Life, Jesus provides all believers with the extraordinary gift of eternal life and the gift of eternal, incorruptible bodies (1 Cor 15:54). When we become Christians, we automatically become citizens of a heavenly kingdom. As a present reality, we experience the Kingdom of God in our lives when we allow Christ, the Messiah to reign as Lord in our hearts and minds.

As we turn to our text, Jesus begins to tell the story of 10 Virgins, 5 who are wise, and 5 who are foolish:

> 25 "At that time the kingdom of heaven will be like ten virgins who took their lamps and went out to meet the bridegroom. ² Five of them were foolish and five were wise. ³ The foolish ones took their lamps but did not take any oil with them. ⁴ The wise ones, however, took oil in jars along with their lamps. ⁵ The bridegroom was

> a long time in coming, and they all became drowsy and fell asleep.

From the onset, Jesus address the issue of readiness, being prepared for the uncertainties of life. The wise virgins bring an extra jar of oil with them as they await the arrival of the Bridegroom. Preparedness, it's a an important virtue in life that helps to avoid unnecessary crisis, by putting into place contingencies. This isn't just a life principal, but a spiritual one as well. How are you preparing to meet Jesus face to face some day?

As our passage continues, there is a major development:

> [6] "At midnight the cry rang out: 'Here's the bridegroom! Come out to meet him!'
> [7] "Then all the virgins woke up and trimmed their lamps.
> [8] The foolish ones said to the wise, 'Give us some of your oil; our lamps are going out.'
> [9] "'No,' they replied, 'there may not be enough for both us and you. Instead, go to those who sell oil and buy some for yourselves.'

The wise virgins are able to trim their lamps and prepare to meet the Bridegroom. The unprepared virgins ask the wise virgins to share their oil. The wise virgins refuse as they are afraid they will not have enough oil for themselves. The unwise virgins must seek out oil in the marketplace. Have you ever been in a situation like the foolish virgins? You failed to plan properly and ended up in a crisis situation? Sometimes this is where we find ourselves and it's not a nice place to be! But what is the meaning of this mysterious parable? What does it specifically teach us about Christian discipleship?

As our passage continues, the five foolish virgins arrive at the wedding feast and knock on the door:

> [10] "But while they were on their way to buy the oil, the bridegroom arrived. The virgins who were ready went in with him to the wedding banquet. And the door was shut.
> [11] "Later the others also came. 'Lord, Lord,' they said, 'open the door for us!'
> [12] "But he replied, 'Truly I tell you, I don't know you.'

> ¹³ "Therefore keep watch, because you do not know the day or the hour.

So the foolish virgins arrive late to the wedding feast and the Bridegroom says "I don't know you." But what is the meaning of this mysterious parable? But what does this teach us about Christian discipleship?

This parable is about the coming wedding feast of the lamb. The Wedding Feast of the Lamb will undoubtedly be the single most important moment in the life of the church. Thus, Revelations 19 says:

> ⁶ Then I heard what sounded like a great multitude, like the roar of rushing waters and like loud peals of thunder, shouting:
> "Hallelujah!
> For our Lord God Almighty reigns.
> ⁷ Let us rejoice and be glad
> and give him glory!
> For the wedding of the Lamb has come,
> and his bride has made herself ready.
> ⁸ Fine linen, bright and clean,
> was given her to wear."
> [Fine linen stands for the righteous acts of God's holy people.]
> ⁹ Then the angel said to me, "Write this: Blessed are those who are invited to the wedding supper of the Lamb!" And he added, "These are the true words of God." (Rev 19:6–9)

Moreover, in the parable, oil is symbolic of the Holy Spirit. The Virgins are required to be full of the Holy Spirit. This is why Ephesians 1:13:

> 13 And you also were included in Christ when you heard the message of truth, the gospel of your salvation. When you believed, you were marked in him with a seal, the promised Holy Spirit, who is a deposit guaranteeing our inheritance until the redemption of those who are God's possession—to the praise of his glory.

The Art of Proclamation

At the moment we first believe in Jesus, the Holy Spirit comes to live in our hearts. The Holy Spirit marks us with a seal, like the royal seals of old, guaranteeing our inheritance in Christ. The wise Virgins are emblematic of those sealed with the Holy Spirit, who live in accordance with agape love. With transformed hearts, we live lives of radical love and service.

As Christians, the Holy Spirit abides in us, helps to transform us into the image of Christ. Good works naturally flow from our transformed souls. We must remember that we are all part of a royal priesthood, called to make sacrifices unto God. These sacrifices consist of worship, good works, the saving of souls and righteous living.

Some of you may be wondering, how can I be like the 5 wise virgins, full of the Holy Spirit? Believe in Christ this day and you shall be saved. This is why Jesus asserted:

> For God so love the world that He gave His only begotten son, that whoever believes in him will not perish but have everlasting life.

Believe in Jesus, whom the Father has sent and as the Bride, you will be like the 5 wise virgins at the Wedding Feast of the Lamb. As the Bride, the church, we will be in perfect union with God. An oh what glorious day that will be. Please pray with me:

> Lord we want to be like the 5 wise virgins, our souls full of the Holy Spirit. Please dwell within us Lord, from this moment throughout all eternity. Be the fire that illuminates our hearts and guides us along the way.

The Parable of the Rich Man and Lazarus

Luke 16:19–31

[19] "Now there was a rich man, and he habitually dressed in purple and fine linen, enjoying himself in splendor every day. [20] And a poor man named Lazarus was laid at his gate, covered with sores, [21] and longing to be fed from the *scraps* which fell from the rich man's table; not only *that*, the dogs also were coming and licking his sores. [22] Now it happened that the poor man died and was carried away by the angels to [a]Abraham's arms; and the rich man also died and was buried. [23] And in Hades he raised his eyes, being in torment, and *saw Abraham far away and Lazarus in his [b]arms. [24] And he cried out

and said, 'Father Abraham, have mercy on me and send Lazarus, so that he may dip the tip of his finger in water and cool off my tongue, for I am in agony in this flame.' [25] But Abraham said, 'Child, remember that during your life you received your good things, and likewise Lazarus bad things; but now he is being comforted here, and you are in agony. [26] And [c]besides all this, between us and you a great chasm has been set, so that those who want to go over from here to you will not be able, nor will *any people* cross over from there to us.' [27] And he said, 'Then I request of you, father, that you send him to my father's house— [28] for I have five brothers—in order that he may warn them, so that they will not come to this place of torment as well.' [29] But Abraham *said, 'They have [d] Moses and the Prophets; let them hear them.' [30] But he said, 'No, father Abraham, but if someone goes to them from the dead, they will repent!'[31] But he said to him, 'If they do not listen to Moses and the Prophets, they will not be persuaded even if someone rises from the dead.' (Luke 16:19-31 NASB)

DURING JESUS' MINISTRY, HE told a famous parable of the rich man and Lazareth, the beggar. Parables were a classic teaching technique of Jewish Rabbis throughout biblical history. Like Aesop's fables of more modern times, every parable had a moral. But just what is the moral of the tale of the rich man and Lazarus the beggar?

Before we begin our examination of this dramatic parable, let's take a look at the use of parables in the ancient world. In biblical times teachers often used short stories to illustrate larger concepts, truths and morals. The parable was a common with Jewish Rabbis. Thus, Jesus used parables to teach others about the kingdom of God. He spoke of the mustard seed growing into a large tree and of tenants of a vineyard holding hostage their master's property. The parable of the rich man and Lazarus fit well within this effective tradition.

As we turn to our text this morning in the gospel of Luke, it's helpful to acknowledge the cultural realities in which Jesus delivers the parable. The Pharisees, one of the major groups of

THE PARABLE OF THE RICH MAN AND LAZARUS

religious scholars among the Jews were known for their love of money and the material comforts and luxuries it provided. In many ways, the parable appears to be a critique of the Pharisees. Thus, one scholar says:

> The Pharisees were accustomed to being in King's houses, in soft raiment, and living delicately. They had attached themselves to Herod Antipas, the Herodians, or those, who differing from them politically, were ready to coalesce with them, and reproduced their mode of life[1].

A full understanding of Jesus' parable is difficult without consideration of these realities.

As we turn to out text, we discover a rich man who is dressed in purple and fine linen. Thus, the text says:

> [19] "Now there was a rich man, and he habitually dressed in purple and fine linen, joyously living in splendorI every day.

In the ancient world, the color purple was very expensive and was worn by the royals in society. It also was worn by high-ranking Roman officers in the military. Fine linen was also very costly and was the choice of the aristocracy and the rich. Luke, our Gospel writer makes it clear that the rich man is wealthy indeed. He is a man accustomed to "living joyously, with a sense of inner triumph, making merry. He lives in splendor every day"[2]. However, the text strongly infers that he is completely self-centered and blind to the needs of the poor.

Next we discover Lazarus, who is poor and suffering. It is a depressing scene. Thus, the text reads:

> And a poor man named Lazarus was laid at his gate, covered with sores, [21] and longing to be fed with the *crumbs* which were falling from the rich man's table; besides even the dogs were coming and licking his sores.

---

1. Discovery Bible, Version 3.0.0, Embros Program
2. Discovery Bible, Version 3.0.0, Embros Program

According to the text, Lazarus is desperately poor and afflicted with sores. He yearns from the depths of his being for just the crumbs from the rich man's table. However, the rich man does nothing to help the beggar, to alleviate his suffering in this life. It is a dreadful scene indeed.

As our passage continues, Lazarus, the poor man dies and his soul is carried by the angels to "Abraham's bosom," a beautiful symbol of blessedness with another, with Abraham in paradise. However, after the rich man dies, his soul is sent to Hades or, an unseen place where the dead reside, the realm of the dead. Thus, the text says:

> [22] Now it happened that the poor man died and was carried away by the angels to [a]Abraham's arms; and the rich man also died and was buried. [23] And in Hades he raised his eyes, being in torment, and *saw Abraham far away and Lazarus in his [b]arms. [24] And he cried out and said, 'Father Abraham, have mercy on me and send Lazarus, so that he may dip the tip of his finger in water and cool off my tongue, for I am in agony in this flame.'

In Hades, the realm of the dead, the rich man is in torment and cries out to Father Abraham across a chasm, that cannot be bridged. He begs for mercy and compassion, that which he never showed Lazarus in his life. Interestingly, the Greek word for torment in this passage refers to a black silicon stone that was used to test the purity of precious metals like silver and gold. Figuratively, it refers to an examination of someone, a difficult test to reveal what is in the heart[3]. The rich man now longs for Lazarus to come and comfort him, to relieve him from the fiery trials of his testing. Thus, our text says:

> But Abraham said, 'Child, remember that during your lifetime you received your good things, and Lazarus in like manner evil things; but now he is comforted here, and you are in agony.
> 16:26 Besides all this, between you and us a great chasm has been fixed, so that those who might want to pass

---

3. Discovery Bible, Version 3.0.0, Embros Program

THE PARABLE OF THE RICH MAN AND LAZARUS

from here to you cannot do so, and no one can cross from there to us.'

The chasm described is like a scene from "Dante's Divine Comedy" with steep rocks and a deep gorge. It is a scene of sharp contrast. On one side of the gorge is an frightful scene of flames the burn but do consume and on the other side a glorious scene of the garden of Paradise with a kingly palace and banquet.

Next the rich man begs Father Abraham to send Lazarus to warn his brothers of such a fate:

> [27] And he said, 'Then I request of you, father, that you send him to my father's house— [28] for I have five brothers—in order that he may warn them, so that they will not come to this place of torment as well.' [29] But Abraham *said, 'They have [d]Moses and the Prophets; let them hear them.' [30] But he said, 'No, father Abraham, but if someone goes to them from the dead, they will repent!'[31] But he said to him, 'If they do not listen to Moses and the Prophets, they will not be persuaded even if someone rises from the dead."

Peter was a busy business manager working in downtown D.C. He often used to have lunch at a nearby Au Bon Pain restaurant. The food was delicious and the customer service warm and friendly. Every day while on the way to lunch he noticed a homeless man sitting near one of the intersections, asking for money. For days Peter was reluctant to help the man, as he thought any money he would give might be used for alcohol or drugs. However, one day filled with compassion for the man, Peter decided to introduce himself and get to know the homeless man. The man said that his name was John-Mark and that he had lost his wife in a terrible car accident. He fell into depression and lost his way in life. He turned to alcohol to bury the pain and eventually lost everything. Peter treated John Mark to a meal in an outside café and they continued to get to know one another. When he returned to his office, Peter had his secretary locate local shelters and community services that could help John-Mark find shelter and begin a road to discovery. John-Mark was accepted into a shelter and a local church partnered with him to secure housing and treatment for his substance abuse problem. Peter stayed in contact with John-Mark, providing emotional and financial assistance in his road to recovery. Peter's compassion harmonizes well with Proverbs 3:27–28 which says:

> Do not withhold good from those to whom it is due, when it is in your power to act. Do not say to your neighbor, "Come back tomorrow and I'll give it to you"—when you already have it with you.

And also Proverbs 31 which says:

> Speak up for those who cannot speak for themselves, for the rights of all who are destitute. Speak up and judge fairly; defend the rights of the poor and needy. (Proverbs 31: 8–9 NIV)

So, what is the moral of the story? Jesus' parable of the rich man and Lazarus illustrates the vital importance of showing compassion and mercy in our lives. Even though the term compassion is conspicuously absent in the narrative, it is the indisputable moral of the story. Christ calls all of us to clothe ourselves with compassion and mercy as we navigate the seas of this life. Like Peter the business manager in D.C. we must reach out with compassion to the poor and the needy. We must not turn a blind eye to the plight of the poor in our midst. For in doing this, we shall be brought safely to Abraham's bosom, our heavenly home, a place of blessedness and peace.

The Parable of the Sower and the Seed

Matthew 13: 1–9, 18–23

13 On that day Jesus had gone out of the house and was sitting by the sea. ² And large crowds gathered to Him, so He got into a boat and sat down, and the whole crowd was standing on the beach.
³ And He told them many things in parables, saying, "Behold, the sower went out to sow; ⁴ and as he sowed, some *seeds* fell beside the road, and the birds came and ate them up. ⁵ Others fell on the rocky places, where they did not have much soil; and they sprang up immediately, because they had no depth of soil. ⁶ But after the sun rose, they were scorched; and because they had no root, they

> withered away. ⁷ Others fell [a]among the thorns, and the thorns came up and choked them out. ⁸ But others fell on the good soil and yielded a crop, some a hundred, some sixty, and some thirty *times as much*. ⁹ The one who has ears, [b]let him hear."
> ¹⁸ "Listen then to the parable of the sower. ¹⁹ When anyone hears the [a]word of the kingdom and does not understand *it*, the evil *one* comes and snatches away what has been sown in his heart. This is the one sown *with seed* beside the road. ²⁰ The one sown *with seed* on the rocky places, this is the one who hears the word and immediately receives it with joy; ²¹ yet he has no *firm* root in himself, but is *only* temporary, and when affliction or persecution occurs because of the [b]word, immediately he [c]falls away.²² And the one sown *with seed* among the thorns, this is the one who hears the word, and the anxiety of the [d]world and the deceitfulness of wealth choke the word, and it [e]becomes unfruitful. ²³ But the one sown *with seed* on the good soil, this is the one who hears the word and understands it, who indeed bears fruit and produces, some a hundred, some sixty, and some thirty *times as much*." (Matt 13:1–9, 18–23 NASB)

THE PARABLE OF THE Sower and the Seed is perhaps one of Jesus' most memorable stories. Jesus, like many rabbis in the Greek and Roman world used the power of storytelling to show contrast between various things or realities. However, its most important point is what it teaches us about prevenient grace, the grace that is with us from the time we are born, that creates good soil in our hearts to receive Jesus, the Word, and to walk in His ways.

Before we begin to explore this exquisite parable in great depth, I want to point out two major ideas in the parable, that are woven into its fabric like a fine garment. First, the seed, the word that is sown refers to not only the spoken word, but also Christ who is the Divine Word who has come into the world as the Light of the World.

The second thread that we see in the fabric of the parable is the idea of grace, or prevenient grace. As you may recall, prevenient grace is the grace of God present in our lives even before

THE PARABLE OF THE SOWER AND THE SEED

we are born that draws us to Christ in our life's journey. Through prevenient grace we have opportunities to respond to the promptings of the God in our lives. It was grace that softened our hearts and made us open to the love of Christ. Through grace, the Lord made the first move and drew us unto Himself.

As we turn to our text, Jesus provides the first example in his comparison of the Kingdom of God to individuals:

> ³ And He told them many things in parables, saying, "Behold, the sower went out to sow; ⁴ and as he sowed, some *seeds* fell beside the road, and the birds came and ate them up.

These are individuals who hear the word of God but do not understand it. When this occurs, the forces of darkness in this world snatch the word from their hearts. Jesus reminds us that we are in a cosmic battle in this life, between the powers of darkness and humanity. Oh how important it is when we preach and teach the Word that we present God's truths with clarity and love. This is why the Apostle Paul instructed Timothy, to study to show himself, approved, a workman rightly dividing the word of God. Sometimes this is easier said than done.

As our text continues, Jesus speaks of the word that falls on rocky soil:

> ⁵ Others fell on the rocky places, where they did not have much soil; and they sprang up immediately, because they had no depth of soil. ⁶ But after the sun rose, they were scorched; and because they had no root, they withered away.

Jesus explains that this is the one who hears the word and immediately receives it with joy; ²¹ yet he has no firm root in himself, but is only temporary, and when affliction or persecution occurs because of the [b]word, immediately he [c]falls away. Jesus makes it clear that in the Christian journey, there will be times when we will experience persecution and affliction because we bear the name of Christ. However, we must never lose heart in our faith journeys.

The Art of Proclamation

We must hold fast to the one who loves us beyond measure and will see use safely home to heaven's shores.

As our text continues, Jesus speaks of Word that falls on thorny soil:

> Others fell [a]among the thorns, and the thorns came up and choked them out.

Jesus explains this is "the one who hears the word, and the anxiety of the [d]world and the deceitfulness of wealth choke the word, and it [e]becomes unfruitful."

The word for anxiety in this passage refers to that which *disunifies* personality, robbing a person of God continuously granting *peace* (His gift of *"wholeness"*). Thus, one scholar says "Anxiety is what causes *part* of us to go *one* way . . . and the rest another! Moreover, the deceitfulness of wealth can render the word unfruitful in our lives. We must never prioritize the quest for wealth over our pursuit of the Kingdom of God. This is why Jesus said seek ye first the Kingdom of God and His righteousness.

As our text concludes, Jesus speaks of the seeds, the Word that falls on good soil:

> But others fell on the good soil and yielded a crop, some a hundred, some sixty, and some thirty times as much. [9] The one who has ears, [b]let him hear."

Jesus explains "But the one sown *with seed* on the good soil, this is the one who hears the word and understands it, who indeed bears fruit and produces, some a hundred, some sixty, and some thirty *times as much.*"

This good soil is a good that comes with understanding, it inspires (motivates) others to embrace what is lovely beautiful, praiseworthy[1]. Many scholars believe this is a goodness, a readiness that is the result of grace in our lives. Grace has always been there, guiding us, making us open to the truth of the Triune God. "Prevenient grace is the grace of the porch. It prepares our hearts and minds to hear and receive the gospel of Jesus Christ, and to

---

1. Discovery Bible, Version 3.0.0, Embros Program

respond in faith"[2]. Ultimately the good soil represents a person, whose heart is touched by grace, who hears, understands, and embraces God's word, ultimately leading to a life that bears spiritual fruit. This heart holds onto the word with patience and perseverance, demonstrating a genuine and lasting faith.

John Wesley taught that God's grace is available to everyone and not just a select few, as some of his contemporaries believed. Unfortunately, many resist God's grace and never choose to come to Christ in faith to continue their spiritual journeys through the door of justification.

This grace harmonizes well with Psalm 51:

> [10] Create [a]in me a clean heart, God,
> And renew a steadfast spirit within me.
> [11] Do not cast me away from Your presence,
> And do not take Your Holy Spirit from me.
> [12] Restore to me the joy of Your salvation,
> And sustain me with a willing spirit.
>
> You do not take pleasure in burnt offering.
> [17] The sacrifices of God are a broken spirit;
> A broken and a contrite heart, God, You will not despise.
> (Psalm 51: 10–12, 16–17)

May God's word always fall on the good soil in our hearts, fashioned by the Holy Spirit. May your hearts, touched by grace yield a crop, some a hundred, some sixty, and some thirty *times as much.*

[9] The one who has ears, [b]let him hear.

---

2. Iovino, "God at Work."

The Wedding Feast

Matthew 22:1–14

22 Jesus spoke to them again in parables, saying, ² "The kingdom of heaven [a]is like [b]a king who [c]held a wedding feast for his son. ³ And he sent his slaves to call those who had been invited to the wedding feast, and they were unwilling to come. ⁴ Again he sent other slaves, saying, 'Tell those who have been invited, "Behold, I have prepared my dinner; my oxen and my fattened cattle are *all* butchered and everything is ready. Come to the wedding feast!"' ⁵ But they paid no attention and went their *separate* ways, one to his own [d]farm, another to his business, ⁶ and the rest seized his slaves and treated them abusively, and *then* killed them.⁷ Now the king was angry, and he sent his armies and destroyed those murderers

and set their city on fire. ⁸ Then he *said to his slaves, 'The wedding feast is ready, but those who were invited were not worthy. ⁹ So go to the main roads, and invite whomever you find *there* to the wedding feast.' ¹⁰ Those slaves went out into the streets and gathered together all whom they found, both bad and good; and the wedding hall was filled with [e]dinner guests.

¹¹ "But when the king came in to look over the [f]dinner guests, he saw a man there who was not dressed in wedding clothes, ¹² and he *said to him, 'Friend, how did you get in here without wedding clothes?' And the man was speechless. ¹³ Then the king said to the servants, 'Tie his hands and feet, and throw him into the outer darkness; there will be weeping and gnashing of teeth in that place.' ¹⁴ For many are [g]called, but few *are* chosen." (Matt 22:1–14 NASB)

THE PARABLE OF THE wedding feast is an intriguing tale about a king whose son is getting married. Like many of Jesus' parables, it contains plot twists and turns that no doubt got the attention of Jesus' audience. However, Jesus doesn't tell a tale for the sake of afternoon entertainment. Instead the parable is a harsh critique of the Jewish elders, Pharisees and other prominent figures. Their rejection of the Lord's invitation to the wedding feast opens new doors for Gentiles to join the Wedding Feast of the Christ and the church. We must clothe ourselves with the wedding garments of holiness to join this feast.

Before we begin to explore our text, let's examine a major theme in the parable. Jesus likens the Kingdom of God to a king who plans a wedding feast for his son. The kingdom of God-just what is the kingdom of God? The Kingdom of God is a both a present and future reality, expanding on the earth through the proclamation of the gospel and the reign of God in the hearts of believers. As the Bread of Life, Jesus provides all believers with the extraordinary gift of eternal life and the gift of eternal, incorruptible bodies (1 Cor 15:54).

During his ministry Jesus spoke of the present reality of the kingdom of God in the world. We experience the Kingdom of God in our lives when we allow Christ, the Messiah to reign as Lord in our hearts and minds. Indeed, the prophet Isaiah spoke of this present and coming kingdom when he wrote:

> ⁶ For unto us a child is born, unto us a son is given: and the government shall be upon his shoulder: and his name shall be called Wonderful, Counsellor, The mighty God, The everlasting Father, The Prince of Peace.

These prophecies about the Messiah speak of Jesus, who is co-equal, co-eternal with God. The Messiah has come to reign in our hearts, to indwell us with the Holy Spirit (Revelations 3:20), to sup with us. We are called to the essence of the God's law, to love the Lord with all of our hearts, souls, minds and strength.

As we turn to our text, Jesus begins to weave his intriguing tale about the kingdom of God:

> 22 Jesus spoke to them again in parables, saying, ² "The kingdom of heaven [a]is like [b]a king who held a wedding feast for his son. ³ And he sent his slaves to call those who had been invited to the wedding feast, and they were unwilling to come. ⁴ Again he sent other slaves, saying, 'Tell those who have been invited, "Behold, I have prepared my dinner; my oxen and my fattened cattle are *all* butchered and everything is ready. Come to the wedding feast!"

Here the king in the parable is the Lord, the Father. He's preparing a wedding feast for his son Jesus. Thus, Revelations 19 says:

> "Hallelujah!
> For our Lord God Almighty reigns.
> ⁷ Let us rejoice and be glad
> and give him glory!
> For the wedding of the Lamb has come,
> and his bride has made herself ready.
> ⁸ Fine linen, bright and clean,
> was given her to wear." (Revelation 19: 6–8)

The King sends out invitations to the Jewish leaders, through the prophets to come to the wedding feast. However, the Jewish leaders ignore the royal invitations. The prophets are persistent in their jobs, but are only met with violence and rejection.

As our text continues, the king responds to the violence of those who have rejected His invitation:

> Now the king was angry, and he sent his armies and destroyed those murderers and set their city on fire. [8]

This is possibly an illusion to the two stage destruction of the Northern and Southern kingdoms of Israel. Despite continuous calls of the prophets for Israel to repent of its idiolatry and sin, Israel continued its sinful ways. Eventually both kingdoms fell into the control of their enemies.

As the parable continues, the King instructs his slaves to go into the roads, the byways and invite strangers to come to the wedding feast:

> Then he said to his slaves, 'The wedding feast is ready, but those who were invited were not worthy. [9] So go to the main roads, and invite whomever you find *there* to the wedding feast.' [10] Those slaves went out into the streets and gathered together all whom they found, both bad and good; and the wedding hall was filled with [e]dinner guests.

Church, this is an important reference to the Gentiles, us. The king is broadening his invitations to all people, all nations, all tongues. Although we once were strangers to the promises of God, we Gentiles become fellow heirs to the kingdom. This is why Ephesians 2 says:

> [19] Consequently, you are no longer foreigners and strangers, but fellow citizens with God's people and also members of his household, [20] built on the foundation of the apostles and prophets, with Christ Jesus himself as the chief cornerstone. [21] In him the whole building is joined together and rises to become a holy temple in the Lord. [22] And in him you too are being built together to become a dwelling in which God lives by his Spirit. (Ephesians 2:19–22)

The Art of Proclamation

As our parable concludes, the King inspects the wedding guests, to ensure they are clothed appropriately:

> [11] "But when the king came in to look over the [f]dinner guests, he saw a man there who was not dressed in wedding clothes, [12] and he *said to him, 'Friend, how did you get in here without wedding clothes?' And the man was speechless. [13] Then the king said to the servants, 'Tie his hands and feet, and throw him into the outer darkness; there will be weeping and gnashing of teeth in that place.' [14] For many are [g]called, but few *are* chosen."

In the ancient world, it was not uncommon for Kings to provide guest to special events, where they were provide special garments for the occasion. The expectation was that one would wear the appropriate clothes. The garments here are symbolic of holiness. Thus, one scholar says:

> "What, then, is the "wedding garment?" Answers have been returned to that question from very different dogmatic standpoints. Some have seen in it the outward *sacrament* of Baptism, some the imputed righteousness of Christ covering the nakedness of our own unrighteousness. These answers, it is believed, are at once too narrow and too technical. The analogy of Scriptural symbolism leads us to see in the "garment" of a man the habits of good or evil by which his character is manifested to others. Here, therefore, the "wedding garment" is nothing less than the "holiness" without which "no man shall see the Lord."

Will you be ready with the garments of righteousness and holiness at the wedding feast of the lamb? Are you in covenant with God and trying to live a holy life? Are you set apart, consecrated, devoted to God? This is what the Lord requires of us. Yes, there will be times when we will fall, but for the most part, of our hearts should long to live for God, to live in accordance with his Word. This is what it means to be clothed in garments of righteousness. Jesus the King provides the garments for the glorious Wedding Feast. Be holy my friends, as your Father in heaven is holy.

Bibliography

Catholic Doors Ministries. "Prayer of Saint Augustine of Hippo." https://www.catholicdoors.com/prayers/english/p00362.htm.

Cerebral. "Agape Love: How to Love Unconditionally." Dec. 5, 2024. https://www.resiliencelab.us/thought-lab/agape-love-how-to-love-unconditionally.

Discovery Bible, Version 3.0.0, Embros Program.

Everhard, Matthew. "Preaching Lab: Voice, Volume, Tone." Jan. 13, 2020. YouTube video, 8:37. https://www.youtube.com/watch?v=bLBsMwqWZnQ&t=12s.

Felton, Gale Carlton. *This Holy Mystery: A United Methodist Understanding of Holy Communion.* Nashville: Discipleship Resources, 2004.

Integrated Catholic Life. "Daily Quote from St. Teresa of Avila, Virgin and Doctor of the Church." Oct. 8, 2011. https://integratedcatholiclife.org/2011/10/daily-quote-from-st-teresa-of-jesus.

Iovino, Joe. "God at Work Before We Knew It: Prevenient Grace." The United Methodist Church (website), Mar. 2, 2018. https://www.umc.org/en/content/god-at-work-before-we-know-it-prevenient-grace.

Just Prayer. "Look Upon Us—St. Augustine." https://www.justprayer.gracespace.info/look-upon-us-o-lord-st-augustine/.

Lindsley, Arthur W. "The Holiness of God." CS Lewis Institute, Sept. 2, 2008. https://www.cslewisinstitute.org/resources/the-holiness-of-god/.

NOAA. "The Water Cycle." Last updated Sept. 26, 2025. https://www.noaa.gov/education/resource-collections/freshwater/water-cycle.

The United Methodist Church. "The Articles of Religion of the Methodist Church." 2016. https://www.umc.org/en/content/articles-of-religion#:~:text=Article%20XVI%20—%20Of%20the%20Sacraments,confirm%2C%20our%20faith%20in%20him.

Willimon, William Henry. *Leading With the Sermon.* Minneapolis: Forest, 2020.

BIBLIOGRAPHY
ART CITATIONS

Fine art photography on pages 9, 15, 25 and 36 were taken by Donald E. Williams. All digital paintings were created using ChatGPT.

www.ingramcontent.com/pod-product-compliance
Lightning Source LLC
Chambersburg PA
CBHW050841160426
43192CB00011B/2116